# Big Beliefs!

## Small Devotionals Introducing Your Family to Big Truths

EDITED BY

## DAVID R. HELM

D1636868

P&R
PUBLISHING
P.O. BOX 817 • PHILLIPSBURG • NEW JERSEY 08865-0817

© 2016 by Holy Trinity Church, Chicago, Illinois

All rights reserved. No part of this book may be reproduced, stored in a retrieval system, or transmitted in any form or by any means—electronic, mechanical, photocopy, recording, or otherwise—except for brief quotations for the purpose of review or comment, without the prior permission of the publisher, P&R Publishing Company, P.O. Box 817, Phillipsburg, New Jersey 08865-0817.

Scripture quotations are from the ESV® Bible (The Holy Bible, English Standard Version®), copyright © 2001 by Crossway, a publishing ministry of Good News Publishers. Used by permission. All rights reserved.

The Westminster Confession of Faith at the back of the book is taken from the *Modern English Study Version* © 1993 The Committee on Christian Education of the Orthodox Presbyterian Church. Used by permission.

Italics within Scripture quotations indicate emphasis added.

ISBN: 978-1-62995-128-7 (pbk)
ISBN: 978-1-62995-129-4 (ePub)
ISBN: 978-1-62995-130-0 (Mobi)

Printed in the United States of America

**Library of Congress Cataloging-in-Publication Data**

Names: Helm, David R., 1961- editor.
Title: Big beliefs! : small devotionals introducing your family to big truths / David R. Helm, general editor.
Description: Phillipsburg : P&R Pub., 2016.
Identifiers: LCCN 2016003937| ISBN 9781629951287 (pbk.) | ISBN 9781629951294 (epub) | ISBN 9781629951300 (mobi)
Subjects: LCSH: Westminster Confession of Faith. | Reformed Church—Doctrines. | Families—Religious life. | Christian education of children. | Christian education— Home training. | Theology, Doctrinal—Popular works.
Classification: LCC BX9183 .B54 2016 | DDC 249—dc23
LC record available at http://lccn.loc.gov/2016003937

*To the children of Holy Trinity Church*

# CONTENTS

## Part Five: The Christian Life

## Part Six: The Church

## Part Seven: The Last Things

# ACKNOWLEDGMENTS

This devotional was first created for the families of Holy Trinity Church Chicago in 2002. I am grateful to the committed core of individuals from Holy Trinity Church who assisted in developing and writing the devotionals. I am also thankful for Ian Thompson of P&R Publishing and his enthusiasm for this project, for Julia Craig for her excellent editorial assistance, and for Helen-Joy Lynerd for helping me to prepare this book for publication. I would also like to thank the Orthodox Presbyterian Church for allowing me to use the modern English version of the Westminster Confession of Faith found in the back of the book.

Finally, I want to acknowledge the children of Holy Trinity Church, Chicago—it is for your salvation that we gladly labor, counting it sweet joy!

David R. Helm
Chicago, January 2016

# INTRODUCTION

## YESTERDAY

About 375 years ago in London, on July 1, 1643, a group of 150 men gathered at the request of the Long Parliament. What these men could not have known then was that they would meet together for five days a week over a period of more than four years. They owe their name, "The Westminster Divines," to the place in which they labored: the Jerusalem Chamber of Westminster Abbey. The majority of the men were Puritan pastors, and they gathered in an effort to stave off a civil war. King Henry VII had declared himself, and not the pope of Rome, to be the head of the church. Therefore, Parliament commanded that this "assembly of divines" put forward, to their best understanding, the Bible's teaching on Christian doctrine, discipline, and church government. What emerged after years of study, debate, and discourse was, in part, The Westminster Confession of Faith.

So influential was their work that the Princeton theologian B. B. Warfield said of it,

> In these forms of words we possess the most complete, the most fully elaborated and carefully guarded, the most perfect, and the most vital expression that has ever been framed by the hand of man, of all that enters into what we call evangelical religion, and of all that must be safeguarded if evangelical religion is to persist in the world.[1]

---

1. B. B. Warfield, *The Significance of the Westminster Standards as a Creed* (New York: Charles Scribner's Sons, 1898), 2.

## TODAY

One of the exalted privileges of the church is the opportunity to help young and eager minds to get an early grasp on Christian doctrine. At Holy Trinity Church in Chicago, we have a commitment to provide fresh gospel resources for our many young families who are attempting to instruct their children in the Christian faith. As evidence of this commitment, we have written and published *The Big Picture Devotional*,[2] a one-year family devotional that traces the plotline of the Bible. That work was our first attempt at teaching biblical theology to kids.

*Big Beliefs!* is a more recent attempt to teach theology systematically to young people. Written for children ages seven through twelve, the devotional guide traces the Westminster Confession of Faith, giving a brief overview of each of the Confession's thirty-three doctrinal headings one lesson at a time. The entire Westminster Confession of Faith is available at the back of the devotional for further study and exploration. If you desire to look more closely at any of the doctrines addressed in a lesson, just look up the parenthetical element that immediately follows the lesson's heading. The number or numbers listed there correspond to the chapter and paragraph numbers of the Confession's summary of that doctrine.

## TOMORROW

Most parents find that doing family devotions with any sense of regularity is difficult. For starters, many young parents never had devotions modeled in the home in which they grew up. On top of that, most parents feel overwhelmed at the notion of doing devotions on a daily basis. They miss a few days, lose heart, and give up. Take heart! *Big Beliefs!* is written to help parents succeed and to help children so that they can face

---

2. David R. Helm, *The Big Picture Devotional* (Wheaton, IL: Crossway, 2014).

tomorrow with courage and conviction. This book can be used in three easy steps:

1. *Commit. Big Beliefs!* only requires three family devotions a week, not seven!
2. *Read.* Simply read aloud to your children the short Bible reading for the day along with the brief devotional paragraph that unfolds the Christian doctrine for that lesson. If you want to refer to the Westminster Confession of Faith, the reference is included in parentheses after the title of the devotional for that day.
3. *Discuss.* Follow up your reading by asking your children the two "Interaction and Reflection" questions that are meant to spur healthy conversation about what you learned that day.

# Part One

# God's Word

IIIIIIIIIIIIIIIIIII *Lesson* 1 IIIIIIIIIIIIIIIIIIII

# THE HOLY SCRIPTURE

## 1 THE RECORD OF REVELATION (1.1)
*1 John 1:1–4*

Abraham Lincoln was one of the greatest presidents our nation has ever known. How much do you know about this man? Where was he born? Was he short or tall? Did he have a wife and children? What was one of the greatest things he accomplished as president? How did he die? Did you ever meet Abraham Lincoln? Do you know anyone who ever met or saw him? The answer to these last two questions is no, because President Lincoln died more than 150 years ago. The only way we can know anything about him is because people who knew him and saw him recorded what they heard and saw in books and other written records. The same thing is true if you want to know about God. In the Bible, you can read about all the things that God did for his people thousands of years ago. As we begin our study through *Big Beliefs!*, remember: the Bible is the only way we can learn about God, ourselves, and God's plan of salvation.

## INTERACTION AND REFLECTION

- In the coming lessons we will be learning exciting stuff about Christian doctrine using the Westminster Confession of Faith. The writers of the Confession began by answering the question "What is the Bible?" Why do you think they started with the

Bible rather than God or people? *(The Bible is where we need to go to learn the answers to other questions.)*

- Take a moment to pray—ask God to reveal great things to you as we study the Bible.

## 2 THE GUIDE TO SALVATION (1.5–7)
*Psalm 19*

What kind of book would you read to learn how to make a pizza? (A cookbook.) What kind of book would you use if you wanted to learn the meaning of a new word? (A dictionary.) Every book has a purpose, and some of our favorite books are the ones that tell an exciting story, like *The Hobbit* or *Charlie and the Chocolate Factory*. What about the Bible? What should we expect to find when we open and read it? Although there are many exciting stories (but no recipes), the primary purpose of the Bible is to teach us about God and his plan of salvation for the world. In the Bible, we read amazing stories about what God did in the past with his people. Best of all, we learn that God sent his Son, Jesus, to save us, and we discover how the good news about Jesus spread to the whole world.

So far we have learned two very important things: first, the Bible is the book that we read to learn about God, and second, it is the book that teaches us about God's plan of salvation.

## INTERACTION AND REFLECTION

- We are going to see two ideas come up again and again in the Westminster Confession of Faith: God is King and Ruler over all (the supremacy of God over all things) and God gets the praise when we are saved (his glory to be received by our salvation). How have these two ideas already been hinted at in these first two devotionals?

- If we didn't have the Bible, how much would we really know about God's being King and Ruler over all and his glorious plan of salvation?

## 3 LISTENING TO THE WORD OF GOD (1.4)
*Deuteronomy 6:1–9*

Did you know that some scientists spend entire days just listening? They use very expensive equipment that allows them to listen to radio waves coming from other parts of the universe. What they hear may one day be used to help other scientists to make important discoveries. As Christians, we believe that we are to listen very closely to what God says in the Bible. We believe that God has spoken to us in the words of the Bible. The Bible is the Word of God. We can be thankful that God has given us his Word, because it reveals everything that God wants us to know about how to live as his people in this world. If you want to know who God is, who we are, and how we come to know God, then pay close attention to the Bible.

## INTERACTION AND REFLECTION

- We have been learning about the Bible. We have discovered how important it is and why we should be thankful to have it. Do you think there is any other book quite like the Bible? What are some questions that you or I might have about life that the Bible can answer?
- If you have small children, today is a good day to sing a song like "The B-I-B-L-E" or "Jesus Loves Me."

# Part Two

# God

IIIIIIIIIIIIIIIIIIIIIII *Lesson 2* IIIIIIIIIIIIIIIIIIIIIII

# GOD AND THE HOLY TRINITY

## 1 THERE IS ONLY ONE GOD (2.1)
*Psalm 145*

What do we mean when we say that there is one God? First, we are saying that God definitely exists. There are some people who do not believe in God at all. Second, we are saying that there is only one God, not two or three or one hundred. In ancient times, most people believed in many gods, and even today some religions believe in many gods, thinking that each of the gods is in charge of a particular area of life. The Bible teaches that there is only one God, and he takes care of everything we need. Third, when we say that there is one God, we are saying that the God we read about in the Old Testament, the Creator of everything and the God of Abraham, Isaac, and Jacob, is the same God we read about in the New Testament, the God and Father of our Lord Jesus Christ. He never changes—he is the same yesterday, today, and forever.

### INTERACTION ⟨AND⟩ REFLECTION

- The writers of the Confession have taught us about the Bible, and now they are teaching us about God. Why do you think they are doing it in this order?
- What does Psalm 145 teach us about God?

## 2 ONE GOD IN THREE PERSONS: FATHER, SON, AND HOLY SPIRIT (2.3)
*Matthew 3:13–17*

Do you think you have to understand something fully before you can know that it is true? I sure hope not! If it were, you would have to fully know how eating an apple makes you stronger before you could say that it is true—or how a light switch works before believing it will make the lights come on.

The doctrine of the Trinity is one of the most important truths in the Christian faith, but it is also one of the most difficult to fully understand. The Bible teaches two important things at the same time: first, God is one; he is not divided into many gods. Second, God has revealed himself as three persons: the Father, the Son, and the Holy Spirit. These three persons in the Trinity work perfectly together, without any arguments or problems. We may not fully understand how it is that there is one God in three persons—but we know enough from the Bible to say that this is true! God is a trinity: three in one.

## INTERACTION AND REFLECTION

- The Bible teaches that God is a trinity. What does this tell us about Jesus?
- How is this different from what Jews or Muslims teach? *(Christianity holds that Jesus is the second person of the Godhead. Jews don't believe that Jesus is God or part of God's plan, and Muslims believe Jesus was just one prophet of many but not the only Son of God.)*

## 3 GOD'S CHARACTER (2.1–2)
*Exodus 34:1–9*

What are some ways you can get to know someone? One way is to introduce yourself and ask them questions about their family and what they like to do. Another way is to spend time with them, because you can tell a lot about a person's character by how they treat others. We should all want to be a person of good character, like God.

In our Bible reading today, we get a glimpse of God's good character. God is both just and merciful. Something happened right before the story we read that made God very upset. His people, the Israelites, made a golden idol to worship. This was a serious act of disobedience. God is the only God, and we must have no other gods but him. Moses prayed to God asking God to forgive the people, and God heard and answered his prayer. In verses 6 and 7, God describes himself as gracious and merciful, someone who forgives the sins of those who are sorry, but also someone who punishes those who are not sorry. This is a wonderful statement about God's character. It shows us that he is merciful toward sinners, yet holy and just in all his punishments.

## INTERACTION ⸻AND⸻ REFLECTION

- How would you define character?
- If God didn't punish bad people, would he be a good God? Why should we be thankful that God is both merciful *and* just?

|||||||||||||||||||||| *Lesson 3* ||||||||||||||||||||||

# GOD'S ETERNAL DECREE

## 1 A GLORIOUS MYSTERY (3.8)
*Romans 11:33–36*

Did you have any choice about where you were born? How about your eye color, did you have any choice in that? Did you have anything to say about what your name would be? Probably not. But there's another question that Christians should ask themselves: Did you have anything to do with the fact that God loved you before you even knew him? No, God loved you before you knew him, and so he loved you before you could even do anything to please him. This is certainly a glorious mystery. God loved us while we were still sinners. We cannot explain why God loved us so much that he sent his Son, Jesus, to live, die, and rise again for our salvation. But even though we can't explain it, aren't you thankful that he did? What does that tell us about God's character?

## INTERACTION ⌐AND⌐ REFLECTION

- Today begins the second lesson of four in which the writers of the Westminster Confession of Faith help us to learn about God. What did we learn about God last time? *(We learned that there is only one God who exists in three persons and his character is both merciful and just.)*

- In this lesson we are learning about God's eternal decree—the idea that God determined all things from the beginning of time and for all eternity. Today we focused on how God loved us before we knew him. Are there other things in your life that you enjoy and are thankful for? Take a minute to thank God for these gifts.

## 2 AMAZING GRACE (3.5–7)
*2 Samuel 9:1–13*

Don't you like reading stories about a person who shows kindness to someone in need? In our passage today, we read about King David's amazing grace toward Mephibosheth, who was the grandson of Saul, the previous king. Saul was David's enemy before Saul died and David became king. It was common in the ancient world for a new king to kill the entire family of the old king so that they could not take the throne. But instead of killing Mephibosheth, King David welcomed him into his house and had him eat at his own table as if he were part of his own family.

There is one more detail in the story that we should notice. David showed kindness to Mephibosheth because David was a friend of Mephibosheth's father, Jonathan. This story is a good illustration of God's grace to us. Though we don't deserve it, God brings us into his house and feeds us at his family table—all because of what Jesus did for us.

## INTERACTION AND REFLECTION

- The Bible teaches that God intended, even before any of us were born, to be gracious to his children by sending Jesus to pay for their sins. How does that make you feel?
- How does the story of David and Mephibosheth illustrate God's love for us?

# 3 PRAISE TO GOD (3.8)
*Psalm 100*

How should you act when you receive a gift? Some people take the gift and leave without thanking the person who gave it to them. Some people take the gift and boast about it to others who did not receive a gift, as if it was something about themselves that made them deserve the gift in the first place. All of us who are in God's family have received a very special gift—the gift of God's grace—which means we have forgiveness of sins and the hope of eternal life.

How should we respond? First of all, we should realize that we did not do anything to deserve God's gift, and so we have no reason to boast about it as if we did deserve it. Second, we should express our thankfulness to God. We can do this with our words, such as the words in Psalm 100, and also with our actions, such as by living in obedience to God's commands. Our words and actions will show the people of the world that God is willing to give this incredible gift to them as well.

## INTERACTION AND REFLECTION

- What are some simple ways you can show praise to God for his gift of Jesus?
- In the next lesson, we will learn a third thing the writers of the Westminster Confession of Faith learned about God from the Bible. Can you recall the two things we have already learned about God? *(We have learned about the Holy Trinity and God's eternal decree.)*

# ||||||||||||||||| *Lesson 4* |||||||||||||||||

# CREATION

## 1 MAKER OF HEAVEN AND EARTH (4.1–2)
*Acts 17:22–31*

The universe that God created is bigger than we can possibly imagine, yet every detail is more complex than we are fully able to understand. Did you know that your own body is made up of millions of cells, each of which is a tiny factory that does a special job to keep you running properly? Did you know that there are about 9.5 million people living in the Chicago area and that if all the people in the world lived in a city the size of Chicago, there would be 737 other Chicago-sized cities in the world?! Earth is one of the smallest of eight planets that circle a sun that is large enough to contain one million Earths. This solar system is only one of billions in our galaxy, called the Milky Way, and this galaxy is only one of billions of galaxies in the entire universe. And we—you and I—are children of the God who made all this.

### INTERACTION ⟨AND⟩ REFLECTION

- In this lesson, we will be learning that our Trinitarian God who decreed all things is also the one who created everything for his own glory. Can you name some things that reflect the greatness of God?
- In our Bible reading today, Paul tells the people in Athens that God is not a manmade image or idol. If God made the heavens

and earth, why would it be silly to worship something made out of wood or stone?

## 2 IT IS VERY GOOD (4.1)
*Genesis 1:26–31*

It is one thing to think about the greatness of God's creation, as we did in the last devotional. But how often do we think of the *goodness* of God's creation? If the earth were any closer to the sun, it would be too hot for life to exist on it, and if it were any farther away, it would be too cold. Everything we need for life springs up from the ground, and the air has just the right mix of gasses to keep both plants and animals living and breathing.

God's creation is very good in another way as well: it is good because it reflects the goodness of God himself. God created the world to display his goodness and wisdom, and he created us for the same reason. When we understand that God did indeed create the universe and everything in it, we can learn so much about God's goodness and wisdom through observing and taking good care of his creation.

### INTERACTION AND REFLECTION

- Where do you see God's goodness displayed in creation? What are some ways you can take care of God's creation?
- God created the heavens and the earth. What does that mean when we think about who is in charge of everything that happens?

## 3 IN HIS IMAGE (4.2)
*Psalm 8*

Who can tell me what the word *apex* means? It means the high point or peak. When God created the heavens and the earth, did you know that human beings were the apex of his creation? The creation story says that

Adam and Eve were the last of God's creations. It was as if everything else was prepared just for them. It was like a surprise party, where all the preparations are made, all the decorations hung, all the food set out, just in time for the guest of honor to show up.

Why were humans considered so special? The psalmist in our passage asked the same question: "What is man that you are mindful of him, and the son of man that you care for him?" (v. 4). The answer is that man—both male and female—was created in the image of God. Each person has an imprint, a stamp, that identifies him or her as one of God's special creations. Being in the image of God means that we were made to worship God with all our heart, soul, mind, and strength, and to rule this world for his glory.

## INTERACTION AND REFLECTION

- All humans are created in the image of God, including those that are not Christians. What are some ways in which even non-Christians show that they are the apex of God's creation?
- Can you think of some people you know who might want to become Christians? Pray right now for an opportunity to tell them about the greatness and goodness of God in Jesus. Jesus is the one human being who perfectly reflects the image of God. That is why he is worthy of being followed.

# IIIIIIIIIIIIIIIIIIIII *Lesson 5* IIIIIIIIIIIIIIIIIIIII

# PROVIDENCE

## 1 THE GREAT SYMPHONY (5.1–3)
*Genesis 50:15–21*

Have you ever seen a ballet or heard a symphony played by an or-chestra? In a good ballet, the dancers never crash into each other even when they are leaping and twirling in all directions onstage. They strictly follow the routine that their choreographer (or dance designer) made them practice over and over again. In a good symphony, each musician follows the conductor's movements. Dozens of musicians play different notes on different instruments, yet the conductor guides each individual musician so that the whole orchestra sounds pleasing to listen to.

In the story of Joseph, God directed the actions of many people, sort of like he was conducting a great symphony or choreographing a dance. Joseph's grand dreams made his brothers jealous, so they sold him as a slave into Egypt. In Egypt Joseph suffered many trials that God used to put him in charge of the whole country, second only to the king himself. Joseph's wisdom helped Egypt and the surrounding regions to survive a terrible famine. During this famine, Joseph's brothers came to Egypt to buy food, and guess who they met? The brother they had sold into slavery years before. Through this complex plot, God provided food for many people, reunited Joseph with his father and brothers, and brought the Israelites into Egypt, where years later God would direct another masterful symphony: the exodus.

## INTERACTION ᔕ AND ᔓ REFLECTION

- Are you surprised at the way God worked so many details out to a good conclusion in today's story? Can you think of a time in your life when God was working things out in a way you did not expect?
- In this lesson we finish Part 2 of the Westminster Confession of Faith. Do you remember what Part 1 was about? *(God's Word.)* How about Part 2? *(God.)*

## 2 GOD CARES FOR ALL (5.7)
*Psalm 104:14–30*

One day Jeremy was thinking of how great his parents were. After all, Jeremy knew that his mom and dad had the weight of the whole family on their shoulders—they made sure Jeremy had the clothes he needed every day, and they made him lunches and helped with his homework. They kept the house clean and worked hard to make money to pay for their home and food and even extra things, like soccer camp and fun family outings to the movies. As he was thinking this, Jeremy's mom came down for breakfast. "Hey, Mom," Jeremy called out, "thanks for taking care of everything around here!"

In this lesson we are learning about God's providence. *Providence* means that God continues to take care of everything he has created. He keeps the sun coming up every morning, he gives rain to the plants and trees, he feeds the animals, and he helps you to grow bigger and stronger every day. If you have noticed, all these things benefit all humans, whether they are Christians or not. God takes care of all his creatures in his providence, even people who do not love him or serve him. God's actions are an example to us. We should do our part in taking care of plants and animals in ways God desires. In the same way, we should do good things for others, whether they are Christians or not.

## INTERACTION AND REFLECTION

- Besides what we discovered in our devotional today, name some other works of God's providence.
- Thank God in prayer for the things you listed.

### 3 FOR THE GOOD OF HIS CHURCH (5.7)
*Romans 8:26–30*

Do you have a hard time believing that good things can come out of bad experiences? Well, it's true. Remember the story of Joseph? Some very bad things happened to him, things that he did not understand. Yet we saw that God was still watching over Joseph and was even using all those bad things to bring about something good. This is true for all God's people, the church. Many things happen to individual Christians or to the church as a whole that look bad and are hard to understand. Just because we are Christians does not mean that everything in our lives will be nice, happy, or easy to understand. Both good and bad things happen to all people, whether they are Christians or not. However, our passage in Romans 8 promises us that no matter what happens to us, God is watching out for us for our ultimate good, just as he did for Joseph and the Israelites.

## INTERACTION AND REFLECTION

- Does God's providence mean that nothing bad will ever happen to us? Knowing the answer to this, how should we respond to God in hard times?
- Can you recite the four things about God that the writers of the Westminster Confession have focused our attention on? *(The Trinity, God's eternal decree, creation, and providence.)* Do you know what they mean?

Part Three

# The Fall, Sin, and Mankind

|||||||||||||||||||||||| *Lesson 6* ||||||||||||||||||||||||

# THE FALL OF MAN, AND SIN AND ITS PUNISHMENT

## 1 THE FIRST SIN (6.1)
*Romans 5:12–21*

Do you like surprises? Some surprises are good, like hearing the music of the ice-cream truck coming down your street on a hot summer day or unpacking groceries and discovering your favorite snacks in one of the bags! Not all surprises are good though. Sometimes we are surprised to find out that what we thought was good was actually bad instead. Adam and Eve must have been surprised in a bad way that day in the garden when they disobeyed God. They thought that eating the fruit would bring them good surprises. Instead, it brought bad things for them—they became sinners who deserved God's judgment. What a sad surprise. But did you know that God wasn't surprised by this? He wasn't. God would use this first sin to show his surprising grace and mercy in sending Jesus to rescue us.

### INTERACTION ✂AND✂ REFLECTION

- What surprises you about the passage we read today? Do you find it comforting to know that God was not surprised by what happened?

- Today we begin Part 3 of *Big Beliefs!* Parts 1 and 2 taught us about the Bible and God. Review what you have learned. In part 3 we will learn about who mankind is, what God has promised to sinners, and who the Son of Man is who has rescued mankind.

## 2 OUR FAMILY RESEMBLANCE (6.2–5)
*Genesis 5:1–5; 6:5–8*

Close your eyes and imagine that it is 95 degrees outside and you are standing next to a swimming pool. But you are not wearing your swimsuit—you are wearing nice clothes like those you have to wear for church. Now imagine jumping into the pool with all those clothes on! You can open your eyes now. Is there any chance that your socks would still be dry? No way! All your clothes would be soaked through. Every part of you would be wet.

Well, the Bible teaches us that when Adam and Eve sinned, every part of them and the creation was soaked through with sin. Nothing was perfect and holy anymore. The Bible reading today also showed us that each person is soaked with sin, that "every intention of the thoughts of his heart was only evil continually" (Gen. 6:5). We need God to help us with sin, don't we? We need him to wash us in something that will undo the damage of Adam's sin.

## INTERACTION ⹂AND⹃ REFLECTION

- Can you think of some ways in which every aspect of your life is "soaked" with sin? Do you think that our Holy God can accept us into his presence just as we are on our own?
- Because we are all descendants of Adam and Eve, we resemble them. That's why we often call Adam and Eve our "first parents." List the ways we resemble our first parents. *(We are humans and sinners like they were.)*

## 3 WHAT WE DESERVE (6.6)
*Psalm 38:1–4*

Here's a tough exercise: try to explain the phrase *Every action has a consequence*. Actions lead to outcomes. For instance, if you jump into water, you are bound to get wet. Can you think of other illustrations?

We have been learning that the first sinful *act* in the garden led to a terrible *outcome* for all of us. Sin brought us a bad surprise. After we soaked ourselves in the pool of sin, God became angry with us. No wonder the psalm we read today has a person praying, "O Lord, rebuke me not in your anger, nor discipline me in your wrath! . . . For my [sins] have gone over my head." In this lesson, we have learned a hard but important truth: we are all sinners, rightly deserving God's anger and wrath. But don't despair! In the next lesson, a happy truth comes to our rescue! God makes a promise to act on our behalf—and his actions in history will reverse the consequences of our own.

## INTERACTION 〈AND〉 REFLECTION

- Do you remember a time when you felt like the psalmist who pleaded with God to forgive him? Be encouraged! In the next lesson we will see the amazing grace of God who makes a promise to rescue us from sin!
- We have a good God who is both just and merciful. Because of our sin, what do we deserve? Because of his mercy, what does God give us instead?

|||||||||||||||||||||||||| *Lesson 7* ||||||||||||||||||||||||||

# GOD'S COVENANT
# WITH MAN

## 1 GOD BRIDGES THE GAP (7.1, 7.3)
*Psalm 111*

When you were a little baby, you were helpless. You could not feed yourself, you could not change your own clothes, and you could not tell your mother if your tummy was hurting. Your parents had to know what you needed, and then they had to provide it for you. We saw in the last lesson that sin breaks our relationship with God. In a way, it makes us as helpless and needy as a little baby. All of us are completely unable to fix the problem that sin causes. God himself must act. Like a loving parent, God knows what we need, and he provides it for us. God's provision of what we need in order to have a relationship with him is what we call a covenant, which is a big word for "promise." As Psalm 111:9 says, "He sent redemption to his people; he has commanded his covenant forever."

## INTERACTION AND REFLECTION

- Because we are helpless to save ourselves, God promises to save us from our sin. How does that make you feel toward God? Does this make you love him more? Why?
- Sin has created a gap between us and God. Why can't we bridge the gap and save ourselves? Why can only God do it? Do you remember what his plan was?

## 2 CHRIST FOR US (7.3–6)
*Isaiah 52:13–53:12*

Do you like taking trips? Where is the most interesting place you have ever been? Mt. Rushmore? New York City? The ocean? The mountains? Or maybe another country? Wherever you have gone, you probably spent the days and weeks before your trip planning, packing, and just thinking about what you would do when you finally got there. On the way to your destination, chances are you asked your parents, "Are we there yet?" Your journey was all about the final destination—the very purpose of your trip.

What is the "final destination" of God's covenant? What is it all about? Our passage gives us the answer: it is Jesus Christ, and everything he has done for us. God has made a covenant with us so that we might receive forgiveness for our sins, peace with God, and eternal life.

## INTERACTION *and* REFLECTION

- What are some of the things our Bible reading today says Jesus provided for us?
- How did he do it? Take a minute to thank God for what he has done for us in Christ.

## 3 THE CHURCH IS OUR CONNECTION (7.6)
*Ephesians 3:1–13*

In the last devotional we talked about our favorite trips we have taken. Sometime during the trip, did you ever ask your parents, "Are we there yet?" If you did, they might have told you to enjoy the ride. Sometimes the ride can be almost as much fun as the final destination, especially if you've ever flown in an airplane. The ride is a good time to learn about and admire the landscape of the country, to read a book or listen to music, or to talk and play with your family.

If the "final destination" in God's covenant is Jesus Christ and all he has done for us, the "ride" is the church, or God's people. The apostle Paul himself said in our passage today that it is through the church that the wisdom of God—Christ—is made known to the world. It is easy for us to overlook the importance of the church in God's plan for our salvation, but just like any trip that you might take, you cannot get to your final destination without the ride. So, enjoy the ride!

## INTERACTION AND REFLECTION

- If the "ride" to our final destination is the church, this means we aren't taking it alone. What are some of the benefits of taking this ride together?
- Why is the church so important? Take a minute to thank God for his people, the visible church which represents his body.

|||||||||||||||||||||||| *Lesson 8* ||||||||||||||||||||||||

# CHRIST THE MEDIATOR

## 1 FULLY GOD AND FULLY MAN (8.2, 8.7)
*Mark 2:1–12*

The paralytic's problem was obvious—he couldn't walk! Yet after his friends let him down through a hole in the roof so that Jesus could heal him, Jesus told him, "My son, your sins are forgiven" (v. 5). What would you have said if you had been that man? Would you have been tempted to say something like, "Thanks a lot, man . . . for nothing! I was hoping for a chance to walk!"

As we read the story, it is easier to see what Jesus was teaching. He wanted everyone to know that he was more than a man who could heal people. It is true that Jesus was a man, but he was so much more! He was God too. And he had the power to forgive sins! Jesus showed the world that he was fully man *and* fully God. He was the Sovereign One *and* the son of Mary, sent into the world to heal us from our sins.

### INTERACTION AND REFLECTION

- Why do you think the writers of the Confession follow up their statements on the fall and God's covenant with a statement on the person of Jesus?
- The Bible teaches us that there is no other way to be forgiven except through faith in Jesus (see John 14:6 and Ephesians 2:8–9). Take some time to confess to Jesus your sin and ask him to forgive you.

## 2 PROPHET, PRIEST, AND KING (8.1, 8.8)
*Psalm 110*

Have you ever been in bed at night and overheard adults talking with one another in another room? It's fun to listen in on their conversation, isn't it? Well, something like that is going on in the psalm we just read. King David is listening in on a conversation that God the Father is having with God the Son. The Father says, "Sit at my right hand, until I make your enemies your footstool" (v. 1). Then David overhears who the Lord will be. He will be the *king*, the one who will rule over his enemies and shatter all other kings. Not only that, but he will be "a *priest* forever" (v. 4). David was so fortunate to hear this. And when David wrote it down, he *prophesied* that this would happen. And do you know what? It did happen! Jesus came into the world as God's Prophet, Priest, and King. Jesus holds all these titles. Jesus is the great Prophet who speaks for God. Jesus is the Priest who makes sacrifice for sin. And Jesus is God's King, the only One we must follow.

### INTERACTION ⟨AND⟩ REFLECTION

- Can you name some of the other roles or names Jesus has?
- Did you know that much of the Old Testament uses the jobs of prophet, priest, and king as pointers to the one true man who would hold all three? Can you think of any Old Testament people, other than David, who held one of these jobs?

## 3 HIS LIFE'S WORK (8.3–5)
*Philippians 2:1–11*

How you would feel if you were an important person in the world? Have you noticed that important people have people standing by ready to serve them? Sometimes important people get used to being waited on hand and foot. Sometimes important people begin to think more highly of themselves than they ought. Even people like you and me, who aren't all that important, expect others to serve us.

In our Bible reading today, we learned that Jesus is not like us. After all, he is God, the most important person in the universe. Yet he didn't stand around expecting others to serve him. No. He left his throne in heaven and became a servant. He died for us self-important sinners. No wonder the Father exalted him to the highest place and gave him the name before which we should bow. The Great One served everyone; therefore, God named him the Greatest One. Shouldn't *we* be serving *him*?

## INTERACTION ⟨AND⟩ REFLECTION

- Read verses 1–5 again. How should we live because of the example of Jesus?
- What are some ways we can be serving Jesus?

# Part Four

# Salvation

|||||||||||||||||||||| *Lesson 9* ||||||||||||||||||||||

# FREE WILL

## 1 WE ARE RESPONSIBLE (9.1)
*Deuteronomy 30:15–20*

Think of some choices you make every day. What to wear, what to eat, or what book to read. Now I am going to give you a choice. Which would you rather have: creamed spinach or pizza? You would choose pizza every time, wouldn't you? The most important choice we face every day is whether to love and obey God or to rebel against him and disobey him. In the passage we just read, Moses tells the people of Israel, "Choose life, that you and your offspring may live, loving the LORD your God, obeying his voice" (vv. 19–20). Sadly, when given the choice between loving God and doing wrong, the Israelites continually chose to disobey. The same is true for all of us. Just like we would choose pizza over creamed spinach nearly every time, we choose to disobey God rather than obey him. God holds us responsible for our choices.

## INTERACTION ✂AND✂ REFLECTION

- Today we begin Part 4 of *Big Beliefs!* Part 4 will last seven lessons. Today is a good day to review what we have already covered. Part 1 was about the Bible. Part 2 taught us about God. In Part 3 we learned about the fall, God's covenant, and Jesus Christ. This lesson we begin learning what the Bible has to teach us about salvation.

- Name some choices you made today. Were any of them wrong? Why do you think you chose the wrong thing? How about asking God to help you obey him tomorrow?

## 2 THE EFFECT OF SIN (9.3–4)
*Matthew 13:10–17*

Have you ever been around someone who spoke a different language? What language was it? When we meet people who speak a language we don't know, we are able to hear the words they say, but we aren't able to understand them. In a similar way, because of our rebellion against God, we aren't able to understand and obey the Word of God. In some ways, God's Word is like a foreign language to us. Jesus sometimes told stories called *parables* to his disciples. Jesus used these parables to teach, but only those who were given the ability by God were able to understand what the stories meant. Parables revealed those who were chosen by God to be his people. We can still see this today, when we see how some people hear the words of the Bible and immediately know they are true, but others hear and think the Bible is false. The Bible teaches that sin has made it impossible for us to understand and obey God's Word. We can do nothing by ourselves to help. God alone gives us new hearts and minds that are able to understand and obey him.

## INTERACTION ⟨AND⟩ REFLECTION

- What is the key to understanding God and his Word? We should approach the Bible with humility and a desire to have God help us. If you find something in the Bible that is difficult to understand, who could you ask for help? *(God in prayer, your parents, your pastor.)*
- Ask God to give you a heart that understands and obeys his Word.

## 3 THE EFFECT OF GRACE (9.4–5)
*Psalm 25:1–15*

What are some signs in nature that tell us that spring is near? The weather gets warmer, it rains more, buds come out on trees, and flowers and birds start to come back. In the previous devotional, we said that sin has made it impossible for anyone to understand and obey God without his help. But did you know there are signs that God is at work helping us? In this psalm, we read of several signs of God's grace—the kind and undeserved help he gives us. When someone chooses to trust in God, that is a sign that God is helping that person. Another sign is that a person asks God to teach them his Word, and he or she begins to understand and obey it. A third sign is that a person asks God for forgiveness. A fourth sign that God is helping a person is that he or she trusts in the goodness and mercy of God alone. Another sign is that a person wants more and more to be near to God in a close relationship. There are many other signs of God's grace. Just like we can see the signs of spring in nature, we can see signs of God's helping people to understand and obey him.

## INTERACTION AND REFLECTION

- What are some other signs of God's grace, or help, in a person's life?
- What signs of God's grace do you see in your own life?

IIIIIIIIIIIIIIIIIIIII *Lesson 10* IIIIIIIIIIIIIIIIIIIII

# EFFECTUAL CALLING

## 1 A WORK OF THE TRINITY (10.1)
*Ephesians 1:3–14*

Do you know how new homes are made? First, an architect designs the house and draws the plan for the new house. Then contractors build the house according to the plan of the architect. Finally, real estate agents bring people to live in the new house. All these people—the architect, the contractor, and the agent—work together to provide homes for people.

Did you know that God accomplishes our salvation in a similar way? First, God the Father planned our salvation before he even made the world. Then God the Son, Jesus Christ, carried out the Father's plans and accomplished our salvation. Finally, God the Holy Spirit sought us out and applied salvation to us. There is one God, who is three persons—Father, Son, and Spirit—and all three work together to bring salvation to us.

Salvation is God's work. We live in the house of God's salvation and all the glory for the house goes to God and not to us.

## INTERACTION ⟨AND⟩ REFLECTION

- If God determined from all eternity to save his people from sin, can anything stop him?

- Today we learned that God seeks out a person, and then changes that person's heart so he or she is saved. If this is true, who should get the credit for our salvation?

## 2 BY GRACE ALONE (10.2)
*Psalm 103*

Can you think of something so amazing and so huge and so unique and so expensive that no one could afford it, earn it, or deserve it? It is hard to think of something, isn't it? But something does fit this description, and the Bible calls that thing *grace*. Grace is one of the amazing qualities of God. Grace is God's free and undeserved favor toward sinners. Because of Jesus's perfect life and sacrifice, God abundantly and generously pours out on us all his many blessings, his forgiveness, and his mercy. Jesus has already accomplished our salvation, so now God sees only Jesus's perfect righteousness when he looks at us. This is very good news! Even though we struggle with sin, God pours out his abundant and generous grace, showering us with his mercy and forgiveness.

No one deserves God's grace and no one can earn God's grace. In fact, God does not need to give anyone grace. So why does God give grace to people? Because he is a gracious God, and he loves us. *Grace* is the thing that is so amazing and so huge and so unique and so expensive that we could never afford it, earn it, or deserve it—and yet we have it!

## INTERACTION AND REFLECTION

- Sometimes we think that we need to become a good person first, and then God will love us. But that is not how God's grace works. How do you receive God's grace?

- Isn't God's grace amazing? Is there anything you can do to afford it, earn it, or deserve it? What does God's grace tell you about his character?

## 3 A NEW HEART (10.1)
*Ezekiel 36:22–32*

I want you to think of a stone. What is a stone like? Is a stone easy to squeeze and form into another shape? Now think of Play-Doh. Play-Doh is easy to squish and shape into lots of different things.

The Bible says that our hearts are naturally like stone. Stones are hard and cannot be reshaped. We cannot change our hearts or mold them into a heart like God's heart; our hearts are set on rebelling against God. That is why the gospel is so powerful and so great. God gives us a new heart, a soft heart, a heart he shapes to be like his own. He gives us a new heart that wants to obey God rather than rebel against him. We learned last time that God gives us grace because he is gracious. One of the gifts of God's grace is a new heart.

Our reading today gave two more reasons why God gives people new hearts. The first is so that he might be shown to be faithful to his promises. The second is so that all the people of the earth might know that he is the only true God. Only God can take sinful rebels with hearts of stone and turn them into obedient and loving people by giving them new hearts.

## INTERACTION 〈AND〉 REFLECTION

- Do you remember some of the signs that show that God is at work in someone's heart? Do those signs make you think that God is at work in your heart?
- Take a moment to pray, asking God for a new heart that is more and more like his.

# ||||||||||||||||||| *Lesson* 11 |||||||||||||||||||

# JUSTIFICATION

## 1 FORGIVENESS OF SINS (11.1, 11.5)
*Psalm 32*

Have you ever traded food with your brother or sister at the dinner table? Maybe you said, "I will take your chocolate cake if you will take my broccoli." Something similar happened on the cross—we call it the great exchange. When Jesus was on the cross, he took all your sin. Then, when you trusted in Jesus, God took all Jesus's holiness and gave it to you. When Jesus died on the cross, your sin was paid for, because death is the payment for sin. Now God doesn't need to punish you; he is free to declare you *justified*.

In the psalm we read today, the writer said that the knowledge that he was a sinner made him feel guilty and far from God. So what did he do? He confessed his sin to God and asked for forgiveness, and God was kind and forgave him. This is really important, because people don't ask for help if they don't think they're in danger. In the same way, before you can ask God for forgiveness, you must know that you are a sinner in rebellion against God and in need of a Savior.

## INTERACTION ⟨AND⟩ REFLECTION

- How would you define the term *justified*? (*To be justified is to be declared righteous in the sight of God: just-as-if-I'd never sinned and just-as-if-I'd kept the law.*)

- Does being forgiven of sin mean you will never sin again? When you sin, what should you do?

## 2 ONLY FAITH IN CHRIST ALONE (11.1–3)
*Ephesians 2:1–10*

Have you seen the child's game that involves putting different plastic shapes into matching holes? Each piece fits through only the hole that was made especially for it. It can be pretty funny to watch a child try to put a round piece through a square hole. What isn't funny, though, is seeing people try to push their way into a relationship with God by using anything other than saving faith. Faith alone saves us from God's anger against our sin. Faith in the death and resurrection of Jesus is the only thing that pleases God. No other thing will fit; no other piece will work. If we want God to declare us justified, we will need faith. In our Bible reading today we saw just that. If we want to be saved, it will be by grace and *through* faith!

## INTERACTION ⫻AND⫻ REFLECTION

- How do people try to justify themselves by means other than faith? *(Good works, being a good person, trusting in their own abilities instead of in Christ's work.)*
- Which person of the Trinity moves us to take hold of Jesus by faith? *(It is the Holy Spirit! Jesus now sits at the right hand of the Father in heaven—the Spirit is here with us.)*

## 3 THIS FAITH IS NEVER ALONE (11.2)
*Judges 7:9–23*

What does air look like? Nothing, because it is invisible. How do you know air is all around you if you can't see it? You can feel it blowing on your face, and you can see it blowing the leaves of trees and moving clouds across the sky. So let me ask you this question: What does faith look like? Although faith is invisible, like air, faith is also like air because you can see it working. In the story we read about Gideon, we can see his faith in his actions. Faith is not merely saying we believe in God, but also living for God. Just as with Gideon, faith comes from God, and God strengthens our faith. How did God strengthen Gideon's faith? He gave a dream to a Midianite soldier and let Gideon hear it. Then Gideon obeyed God in the strength of his faith by defeating the Midianites. God is at work today as well, strengthening our faith in him so that we might obey him.

## INTERACTION AND REFLECTION

- Try illustrating faith by closing your eyes and letting someone catch you as you fall backward.
- Can others see your faith? Think of some of the ways faith can be seen. *(Submitting to God and other human authorities and suffering for the gospel are two great examples.)*

# IIIIIIIIIIIIIIIIIIIII *Lesson 12* IIIIIIIIIIIIIIIIIIIII

# ADOPTION

## 1 A NEW FAMILY (12.1)
*Ruth 1:6–18*

How do you know you are part of your family? This is kind of a crazy question, but think about it. You have the same last name as your mom and dad, you live in their house, and they take care of you. If you were born into your family, you probably look like your parents. But maybe you were adopted, or maybe you know someone who was adopted. In adoption, a family takes a child whose mother and father are not able to raise him or her and makes that child a real part of their family forever. The child comes and lives in a new house, receives a new name, and has a new father and mother. The new father and mother promise to love and care for their new child. An adopted child has all the rights, responsibilities, and privileges of any other child, except he or she may not look like his or her new parents very much, like Ruth in the story we read. She said that she would be part of Naomi's family, live with her, and serve God with her. Did you know that everyone who believes in Jesus is adopted into his family? We can call God our Father, he promises to care for us, we live in a new family called the church, and we have a new name, "Christian."

## INTERACTION 〈AND〉 REFLECTION

- The writers of the Confession want to teach us about salvation, and to do so they show us what the Bible says about salvation. Look at the titles of the last few lessons to see the steps they have taken so far. Can you and your parents describe each one in your own words? *(Free will to effectual calling to justification.)*

- In this lesson, we learn what it means to be adopted into God's family. Thank God for adopting sinners into his family as sons and daughters.

## 2 A LOVING FATHER (12.1)
*1 John 2:28–3:10*

Have you ever noticed that children want to please their parents? Children naturally want the love and approval of their parents, even though they may not always obey their parents or do what is right. All this is so because children love their parents. The Bible teaches that God is our Father and that children of God will want to please their heavenly Father because they love him. Why do you think God's children love God? In the passage we read, we learn that our love for God comes from his love for us. God loves us and has placed us into his family and promised us a new home in heaven. Because we know God's love and hope one day to be with him forever, we ought to do what pleases him while we live on earth. True children of God, although they will not always do what pleases their heavenly Father, will want to live in a way that gives him great joy.

### INTERACTION AND REFLECTION

- What are some things that make our Father God really happy?
- How are we able to love God and others? *(God first loved us.)*

## 3 A GLORIOUS INHERITANCE (12.1)
*Psalm 23*

What happens to people's stuff—like cars, houses, boats, motorcycles, and computers—when they die? Normally, if people have children, they leave all their stuff to their kids. The stuff they leave is called an *inheritance.* Usually, kids get to enjoy their parents' stuff right now, a long time before their parents die. In this lesson we have learned that God has adopted us into his family. As God's children, we have an inheritance that we get to enjoy even while we live on the earth. The psalm we read today helps us to better understand our inheritance by looking at two roles God fulfills in our life: a shepherd and a host. A host shows hospitality to others. In this psalm, the host prepares a banquet table for others to enjoy. As our Shepherd, God leads us, protects us, provides for us, and gives us rest and peace. Because he is our Father, we can also trust that no matter what happens to us in life, God is caring for us according to his goodness and mercy. Because we have been adopted into God's family forever, we know that when we die we will inherit eternal life—the greatest inheritance of all.

## INTERACTION *and* REFLECTION

- Does being adopted into God's family mean Christians will never have difficulties or enemies? Look back at the psalm for help.
- What do you think heaven will be like? Take time to think on the eternal inheritance God's children have.

# ||||||||||||||||| *Lesson 13* |||||||||||||||||||

# SANCTIFICATION

## 1 THE BATTLE BEGINS (13.1)
*Psalm 51:1–13*

Psalm 51 began on a rooftop. One spring day, instead of being out in battle like other kings, King David was home, taking a walk on his flat rooftop. When he saw beautiful Bathsheba bathing nearby, he decided he wanted her for himself. So he committed adultery (took another man's wife) and then, to cover up his sin, he had her husband, Uriah, killed. Later, after he was confronted with his sin, he wrote Psalm 51 as a prayer of repentance. This psalm focuses on David's need to have God cleanse him from sin. Sanctification is the battle that Christians fight with sin. Even though we who believe in Jesus have the Holy Spirit, we still live in our flesh (our sinful human nature). Fortunately, God works in us to cause us to grow more like Jesus. This is a lifelong battle that only God can win, but our job is to fight alongside the Holy Spirit against our sinful desires.

### INTERACTION AND REFLECTION

- Read Philippians 2:12–13. According to Paul, who is it who "works" on our lives so we are made more like Jesus?
- How does David's attitude toward sin help us in our "battle" of sanctification?

## 2 A LIFELONG BATTLE (13.2, 13.3)
*2 Peter 1:3–11*

Think about the work people have to do to have a nice yard: they have to mow the grass, rake leaves, and weed the garden. Have you ever had to do yard work? It can be tiring and difficult work, and there will always be more work to be done, if not today, then tomorrow or next week, as the grass and weeds grow or leaves fall. We might ask, "Can't I be done yet?" As Christians, we sometimes forget that the Christian life is often tiring and difficult work. Our last devotional introduced the idea that the Christian life is a battle. Today we take a look at the kind of hard work, energy, and fighting it takes to overcome our flesh and pursue holiness. Peter tells us that it will require our "every effort" (v. 5). It requires self-control, steadfastness, and godliness (v. 6). Thankfully, we have the Holy Spirit to help us! Many of us want the Christian life to quickly become easy. But biblical Christians are diligent and hardworking. Remember, your hard work and the help of the Holy Spirit can result in a soul that looks like a well-manicured yard!

## INTERACTION AND REFLECTION

- Look back at the passage we read, and tell me what God is doing and what we should be doing. What does this tell us about the battle we are facing?
- How can we help each other fight to overcome sin in our lives?

## 3 GROWTH IN GRACE (13.1, 13.3)
*Jonah 1:17–2:10*

When we are trying hard at something, we all like it when someone says, "Hey, you're getting much better at that! I see your progress." The good news about sanctification is that we do make progress. The Confession says that those who have a new heart are helped along in growth by the Holy Spirit. The prophet Jonah is a wonderful example of this—God sought him out and was patiently committed to his growth. Although Jonah lived long before Christ, it is clear that he also was in need of God's further work, and that his own sinfulness got the best of him. In our passage today, Jonah intentionally ran in a different direction than God had told him. It took God's appointing a fish to swallow him before Jonah was ready to call upon God in distress. This was God's way of helping Jonah grow toward perfect holiness.

## INTERACTION $\text{AND}$ REFLECTION

- In the story of Jonah, how effective were God's actions in reversing Jonah's disobedience? Why do you think that God went to such great lengths for Jonah?

- The past five lessons have explained many exciting things about salvation. In the next lesson we will see how God saves sinful people; we will see the fruit of the Spirit's effectual calling; and we will see what it is that gives us justification, adoption, and sanctification. The answer will be *saving faith*.

IIIIIIIIIIIIIIIIIIIIIIII *Lesson 14* IIIIIIIIIIIIIIIIIIIIIIII

# SAVING FAITH

## 1 A GIFT OF GOD (14.1)
*Psalm 22:1–11; Ephesians 2:8–9*

Think about a young baby. What are some things that a baby can do? Not much! If the baby is very, very young, basically the only thing he or she can do is eat and sleep. Babies are content to simply be held in their mother's or father's arms. Yet listen to what David, the psalmist, says here in Psalm 22:9: "You made me trust you at my mother's breasts"! What David is saying is amazing because it means that even when David was still being fed by his mother, God allowed David to trust in him. Faith for anyone is a gift, whether they are a young child or an adult. In Ephesians, Paul (like King David) also emphasizes that salvation and faith are gifts from God. However, Paul describes us as even more helpless than a baby when we receive salvation—he says we are "dead in [our] trespasses and sins" (Eph. 2:1). What both passages teach us is that saving faith is always a gift from God. It is trust in the wonderful death and resurrection of Jesus Christ for our sins.

### INTERACTION ⟨AND⟩ REFLECTION

- Certainly not every person has faith at the youngest of ages. Can you remember a time when you did not have faith in the death and resurrection of Jesus?
- How easy is it for you to think of saving faith as a gift from God?

## 2 A HAND THAT RECEIVES (14.2)
*Genesis 12:1–9*

What does it take to receive a gift? The answer is not money, or work, or anything that begins with you. The most important thing it takes to receive a gift is a *giver!* Someone has to be giving a gift. After that, all that is needed to receive a gift is an open hand. Isn't that what happened with God and Abraham? God was the giver of some amazing gifts that he promised to Abraham. Abraham did not pay or work for the promises God gave to him—all he did was receive what God promised, like a little child who reaches his hands up to receive something from someone kind. What does it take to receive a gift? A giver and a hand that receives. So it is with God's gift of faith, and so it is with salvation. God offers salvation to us. We simply receive his gift with faith, like Abraham did.

## INTERACTION AND REFLECTION

- Would you rather receive a gift or work hard for something? Why?
- Spend a few minutes asking God for open hands that are ready to receive the gift of saving faith.

## 3 LIKE A MUSTARD SEED (14.3)
*Matthew 17:14–21*

Let's take a second to think of some things that are small and strong:

1. *firecrackers*, because they have gunpowder in them
2. *ants*, because they can lift things that weigh much more than they do
3. *mustard seeds,* because they are tiny, tiny seeds that grow into large trees

All three of these things are small and powerful.

When Jesus talks to his disciples in this passage, he chooses a mustard seed to teach them about faith. He wants them to know that even the smallest faith can accomplish something mighty. Why? Not because of faith but because of God. This is a comfort to us! Our faith may not feel big or strong, but if we believe in Christ and his gospel, then our faith is *there*. It is real. And even though our faith may be weak or small, the One we have faith in is very, very powerful.

## INTERACTION ✄AND✄ REFLECTION

- How big is your faith?
- Tell me which question is more important: "How big is your faith?" or "In whom has your faith been placed?"

|||||||||||||||||||||| *Lesson 15* ||||||||||||||||||||||

# REPENTANCE UNTO LIFE

## 1 HATRED OF SIN (15.2)
*Genesis 39:6b–12*

Is there someone that you would like to grow up to be like? How about Joseph? He is a great picture of a person who hated sin. He literally ran away from it, turning away from Potiphar's wife toward God. Can you picture that? Running from one thing and toward another? This is what repentance is: repentance is turning away from sin and toward God. The Bible teaches that when a person repents, they turn away from their sins not only because of the danger of God's judgment but also because they hate the filth of their sins. Repentance means even grieving for those sins (15.2). The prophet Joel records God's calling us to repentance: "'Yet even now,' declares the LORD, 'return to me with all your heart, with fasting, with weeping, and with mourning; and rend your hearts and not your garments'" (Joel 2:12–13). Repentance means hating sin as much as God does.

## INTERACTION ⟨AND⟩ REFLECTION

- The writers of the Confession want you to know that saving faith and repentance go side by side. One is always with the other. Can you think of why these two things are linked together?
- How much does God's heart hate sin? Why should we desire repentant hearts?

## 2 CONFESSING OUR SIN (15.4, 15.5, 15.6)
*Psalm 116*

In our last devotional, we talked about the first step in repentance, which is hating our sin. Today we learn the second step: confessing our sin. David says that when he kept silent about his sin, his bones "wasted away" and his "strength was dried up as by the heat of summer" (Ps. 32:3–4). It is not enough to hate sin; we must also confess our sin to God. Confession is the part of repentance where we describe to God the things that we have done wrong—and ask for forgiveness. The writers of the Confession make a few important points about confessing and repenting: first, that *no sin is too small to confess*, because any sin deserves punishment (15.4); second, that we ought to repent not just *generally* but also of every *particular* sin that we can (15.5); and third, that we ought to confess our sins not only to God but also to *any person* whom we may have hurt or offended and to ask for their forgiveness (15.6).

## INTERACTION AND REFLECTION

- What are some of the things that keep you from confessing your sins to God?
- Spend some time quietly confessing some of your sins to God.

## 3 STRENGTHENING OF PURPOSE (15.2)
*2 Timothy 2:1–13*

Today we come to the third step in repentance, which could be called "strengthening of purpose." First, we must hate sin; second, we must confess it; and third, we must decide to stay away from sin. Think about a soldier. What words describe a soldier to you? *Disciplined, brave, devoted.* Those are good words. Another word could be *focused.* A soldier doesn't get tangled up in everyday things of life. He or she must stay away from those kinds of things in order to be ready for war at any time. Paul teaches that just as a soldier does not get tangled up in everyday matters, you and I are to keep ourselves untangled from sin so that we can serve God. This is a very important part of repentance—being strengthened in grace.

## INTERACTION *AND* REFLECTION

- Which is hardest for you: hating sin, repenting of sin, confessing sin, or staying away from sin? Ask the Holy Spirit to help you with this.
- Today we finished Part 4 of *Big Beliefs!* Do you remember the seven aspects of salvation that the writers of the Confession wanted you to learn from the Bible? What do each of the aspects mean? *(Free will, effectual calling, justification, adoption, sanctification, saving faith, and repentance.)*

# Part Five

## The Christian Life

IIIIIIIIIIIIIIIIIII *Lesson 16* IIIIIIIIIIIIIIIIIII

# GOOD WORKS

## 1 COMMANDED BY GOD (16.1, 16.2)
*Matthew 5:13–16*

Have you ever been in a thunderstorm when all of a sudden the lights went out? Maybe you had to scramble around the house to find a flashlight or even a candle. If you found a candle, you may have held it high and put it in the place where the light would help you to see best. Jesus says some amazing things in our reading for today. He says that Christians are the light of the world. They help other people to *see* that God is real when they do good works. In fact, Jesus commands us to do our good works so that people will glorify God who is in heaven.

### INTERACTION AND REFLECTION

- The writers of the Westminster Confession of Faith thought carefully about what they wanted to say and how they wanted to say it. In Part 1, they covered the Bible. Part 2 was on God. Part 3 looked at the fall, sin, and mankind. Part 4 was an extended look at salvation. Here in Part 5 it makes sense that we look at the Christian life next.

- Let's think hard for a minute: What are some of the good works that Jesus has in mind for us to do?

## 2 EVIDENCE OF TRUE FAITH (16.2, 16.3)
*Psalm 26*

Have you ever had the chance to pick berries or apples? It is a fun thing to do! You get a container to place the fruit in and carefully choose fruit that seems ripe. If you come to an apple or berry tree with no fruit and no green leaves, what does that tell you about it? Most likely it is dead!

Our Confession and the Bible teach that our good works, like fruit, show whether our faith is dead or alive. If we say that we have faith, but no good works, the Bible says that our faith is dead (James 2:17). The psalm we read today shows us the life of someone who is alive—someone who has evidence of true faith. What does that person do? He or she walks in God's truth.

## INTERACTION *AND* REFLECTION

- Does your Christian life show how thankful you are to God for saving you? What ways can you show God your thanks?
- The Bible teaches that we are "created for good works" (Eph. 2:10)? How should that make us feel?

## 3 ALL FOR THE GLORY OF GOD (16.2, 16.7)
*Exodus 19:1–6; 1 Peter 2:9*

Have you ever collected things or held on to something special? What was it? Why did you collect it? Wasn't it because it was something special to you—something you treasured? This may sound strange, but the very reason why God keeps his people is because they are a treasure to him. Exodus says that God's people were to be his "treasured possession" (v. 5). Our reading from 1 Peter says that his people were saved as "a chosen people, a royal priesthood, a holy nation, a people for his own possession, *that you may proclaim the excellencies of him* who called you out of darkness into his marvelous light." Our lives and our good works really have one purpose—to bring pleasure and glory to God. Just like we talked about a few days ago—our lives are to shine, but they shine to give God glory.

## INTERACTION AND REFLECTION

- Is it easy or hard to believe that you are "God's treasured possession"?
- God wants to be glorified, and we should want to glorify him too. How can we use our good works to glorify his name?

|||||||||||||||||||||||| *Lesson 17* ||||||||||||||||||||||||

# THE PERSEVERANCE OF THE SAINTS

## 1 GRACE IS STRONG (17.2)
*Psalm 121*

Have you ever fallen down? Of course you have! Did you get up? Of course! Everyone has stumbled at some point in his or her life. Getting up and keeping on going is called *perseverance*. Imagine if we fell down and never got up—we just lay there! The writers of the Confession teach us in this lesson that those who are called by God and sanctified by his Spirit will always get up and keep going in the race. Even better than that, Psalm 121 teaches that God is the one who helps us keep going. Look at the passage and list some of the things that it says about God's help for us: Our help comes from him (vv. 1–2); he is the Maker of heaven and earth (v. 2); he will not let our foot slip away (v. 3); he is never asleep on the job (v. 4); and he will keep our lives (v. 7). Knowing how strong God's grace is helps us to remember that he is the one who gives us the strength to persevere.

## INTERACTION AND REFLECTION

- Considering that God is the one who keeps us going, and that he is Ruler and King over all, do you think that all true Christians will finish the race of salvation?
- What if someone seems to have stopped running the race? What should we do if we stop?

## 2 GOD'S CHILDREN WILL ENDURE (17.1)
*Daniel 3*

One of the amazing things about the people of God is what they will endure for him. Very often we hear in the news these days of Christians who endure great suffering and even death for God. Hebrews 11 lists all the things that Christians endured to identify themselves with Christ (vv. 36–38). Some were tortured; others were stoned, sawn in two, or killed with the sword. Today in Daniel we read of the great endurance of Shadrach, Meshach, and Abednego. They endured the burning fiery furnace rather than worship the image of gold that Nebuchadnezzar had created. What do we learn from this? That God's children will endure! Those who are truly his children are willing to persevere through very difficult circumstances, just as Shadrach, Meshach, and Abednego did.

## INTERACTION *and* REFLECTION

- Do you think it was hard for Shadrach, Meshach, and Abednego to tell the king that they would not bow down to worship the image of gold?
- What helped them to endure such difficulty? How might knowing this help you?

## 3 NO SHRINKING FAITH (17.3)
*Hebrews 10:32–39*

Have you ever been so startled by something that it caused you to shrink back in fear? People get startled by many things that cause them to shrink back: an animal that unexpectedly darts out in front of them, or even a family member who comes around the corner and catches them off guard. In the passage we read today, the author tells God's people, "Don't shrink back! Remember your confidence—and if you do, you will have a great reward!" The author reminds them of the confidence they used to have and encourages them to keep working hard and enduring. The people were tempted to shrink back; they wanted to go back to trying to establish a relationship with God in a way that would have made other people accept them instead of bullying them. The book of Hebrews teaches us an important lesson. We *must* endure and persevere so that we finish our lives well. We are not to shrink back! You need to persevere so that, when you have done the will of God, you will receive what he has promised. God has done a wonderful thing for us through his son, Jesus. Are you still running in faith, or are you shrinking back?

## INTERACTION and REFLECTION

- Describe how you plan to run the race that is set before you (Heb. 12:1–2).
- What do you think "shrinking faith" looks like? Take a minute to pray that you won't have shrinking faith.

|||||||||||||||||||||| *Lesson 18* ||||||||||||||||||||||

# THE ASSURANCE OF GRACE AND SALVATION

## 1 THE FAITHFUL CAN BE ASSURED (18.1)
*Romans 8:31–39*

Imagine three kids hiking in the mountains on a hot summer day. They have seen on a map that a refreshing lake for swimming lies just over the distant ridge. But having never been there—and with some hard walking still ahead of them and the afternoon sun beating down on them—they begin to wonder if the lake really exists. They have doubts.

The Christian life can be like that too. Having read in the Bible that God will save from sin everyone who believes in Jesus, and hearing that heaven awaits us just over the ridge of this life, we set out in faith. But in the oppressive trials and worries of life, doubts emerge.

It is natural to have doubts and to feel like your faith is small. We can take heart because there is good news for us in our Bible reading today. Paul speaks with great confidence about the eternal destination of the faithful. He says that nothing can "separate us from the love of God in Christ Jesus our Lord" (Rom. 8:39). This lesson's devotionals will give you two ways that you can be assured this is true.

### INTERACTION ✂AND✂ REFLECTION

- Do you find it comforting to learn that doubts are natural in Christian life? Why or why not?

- Through prayer and the work of God you can gain assurance from doubts. What are some words you could pray if you were having doubts about God and his plan?

## 2 GOD KEEPS HIS PROMISES (18.2)
*Joshua 1:1–9*

Julia had a worried look on her face as she sat at the kitchen table one fall morning. Her family had moved to a new city, and today was the first day of school. On top of this, Julia would be riding the bus for the first time. Her father kneeled down beside her and said, "Julia, I know you are scared, but don't be afraid. I'm not asking you to do something that I haven't already scouted out ahead of time. Your bus driver's name is Mr. Cartwright, and your teacher's name is Ms. Dickinson. Both of them are looking forward to meeting you. Remember, I have already found out everything about the school and your teachers. I'm with you in this new adventure. OK?" Listening to her father's words gave Julia some assurance that everything would be all right. So it was with Joshua too! God's words gave him all the assurance he needed to go into the Promised Land. Trusting in God's Word can give you assurance of entering into heaven. His Word is true! Believing in the truthfulness of God's Word is the first way to gain assurance of salvation.

## INTERACTION AND REFLECTION

- Does assurance come from trying to feel confident inside or by believing God's words?
- Does God keep his promises? Why is this comforting to know?

## 3 THE HOLY SPIRIT HELPS US (18.3, 18.4)
*Psalm 143*

Sometimes we wake up in the middle of the night. That can be frightening, can't it? The room is dark, the house or apartment we live in is really quiet, and tomorrow's sunrise seems to be a long way off. In their own funny way, our minds can almost trick us into thinking that a new day won't come at all.

Did you know that we experience the same kind of funny thoughts in our spiritual life too? It's true. We all do. The psalmist in our reading today has doubts about whether God will rescue him from his fears and worries. He needs God's help because his confidence that God is with him is shaken. He feels like God is making him "sit in darkness" (v. 3). But then he prays, "Let your good Spirit lead me" (v. 10). We should do the same thing when we begin to think that God's promises aren't true. We should call on his Spirit to lead us. The Holy Spirit is the second way God gives us assurance of our salvation. God put his Spirit in us, and his Spirit reassures us in times of doubt.

## INTERACTION ⟨AND⟩ REFLECTION

- The writers of the Confession want us to know that God's Spirit is ultimately the one who confirms the work of God in our hearts. This is what the Bible teaches. Thank God for the Holy Spirit.
- Can you name the two ways God helps us to overcome our doubts and fears? *(Through his Word and his Spirit.)*

||||||||||||||||| *Lesson 19* |||||||||||||||||

# THE LAW OF GOD

## 1 GOD'S WILL FOR ALL (19.2, 19.5, 19.6)
*Psalm 1*

Sometimes someone asks a question to get conversation started. Today I have just such a question: "What do you want out of life?" A host of good answers are out there: happiness, adventure, good friends, a loving family, lots of opportunities. These are all good answers, but did you know that today's Bible reading gives us an answer big enough to include all these things? Psalm 1 uses the word *blessed*. Blessed means "approved by God"! Imagine, at the end of life, that God calls you "blessed"—approved—worthy to stand in his presence after the final judgment. If that happens, you will get a long life, a healthy life, a life filled with eternal opportunity and happiness. But did you hear what kind of person receives this kind of life? In verse 2 we read, "his delight is in the law of the LORD, and on his law he meditates day and night." God kindly gave us his law to read and obey. His law helps you to get the most out of this life . . . and the next!

## INTERACTION ⟨AND⟩ REFLECTION

- What would it look like if we loved God's Word the way the psalmist does?
- Why is the blessed life the best kind of life? What do you think a blessed life looks like?

## 2 THE BLESSED LIFE (19.6)
*Exodus 24:1–11 and Matthew 5:17–19*

I want to ask you two crazy questions: Can you walk along a path that isn't really there? Can you listen to your parent read you a book that hasn't even been written yet? The answer to both these questions is no, isn't it? For you to do those things, someone else first needs to make a path or write a book. This also applies to living the blessed life God intended for us. We couldn't walk in God's way if he hadn't shown it to us. We can't hear his voice if we don't read what he has written to us in his book. In our first Bible reading today, we learned that God spoke his words to Israel after he rescued them from Egypt. They needed his words in order to be his people in the world. In our second reading, Jesus warns his followers not to forget to follow God's law. The same is true for us. If we want to live a life that is blessed—that is, approved by God—then we will pay close attention to God's written Word.

## INTERACTION *and* REFLECTION

- Some people think they can follow Jesus without paying much attention to reading, understanding, and obeying the words of the law. Do you think they will live a blessed life? Why not?
- God gave Israel his Law *after* he rescued them as his people. Thank God that his Law is his gracious word to his people.

## 3 WHAT GOD REQUIRES, HE PROVIDES (19.7)
*Hebrews 4:11–16*

Did you ever get a toy on your birthday or at Christmas that required batteries? Did the batteries come with it? It's frustrating when a toy that was intended to bring you great joy goes unused because someone forgot to include the power needed to run it. God did not give his children the great gift of salvation without including the power to obey his Son and his Word. The law of God, which God gave you to live an approved life, comes with the power pack necessary to live it out. God includes the "battery" of his Holy Spirit to make you not only desire to obey God's Word, but also to cherish it and live it out with great joy. What a wonderful truth! God the Father provides us with everything we need to be his people. He gives us his law, his Son, and his Spirit.

## INTERACTION AND REFLECTION

- People often think we obey God's Word in order to win God's blessing. How is this different from what Scripture teaches— that we obey God's Word because we have his Spirit?
- Take a minute to thank God for his Spirit and to ask his Spirit to help you to live an approved life.

IIIIIIIIIIIIIIIIII *Lesson 20* IIIIIIIIIIIIIIIIII

# CHRISTIAN LIBERTY AND LIBERTY OF CONSCIENCE

## 1 FREEDOM FROM FEAR (20.1, 20.2)
*Psalm 27*

If there's one person who strikes fear into our hearts on the playground, it's the school bully. Bullies try to intimidate us, don't they? Just because they are bigger and stronger, they think they have control over us. However, the person who takes our fears away is someone who protects us from the bully—as if he or she were our own big brother or sister. With our protector around, we are free to play and enjoy everything around us.

Did you hear what the psalmist says in our Bible reading today? He says, "The LORD is my light and my salvation; whom shall I fear . . . of whom shall I be afraid?" (v. 1). There is no fear in his heart anymore! He knows that someone bigger than a bully is protecting him. So it is with us. Jesus protects us. We don't need to live in fear any more. Even though we disobeyed God's law and Satan would like to bully us around, he no longer controls us. In Christ, we are free to live life to the fullest, celebrating God's goodness and enjoying him forever!

### INTERACTION ⌦AND⌫ REFLECTION

- Because of Christ's perfect life and sacrifice on our behalf, God has freed us from trying to be good enough to get to heaven. How does this make you love God even more?

- Even though Christians are free from the wrath of God in Christ, Satan will still try to fill us with fear, especially when we sin. Should we continue to be afraid of Satan's bullying? Why? Why not?

## 2 FREEDOM TO SERVE GOD (20.1, 20.3)
*Exodus 19:1, 4–6; 20:1–17*

What does it mean for a person to be *free*? Sometimes it is easier to understand a word if we think about its opposite. When the Israelites lived in Egypt they were the opposite of free—they were slaves, forced to do jobs they did not want to do, and they were not allowed to leave. Then one day, God set his people free. They stopped the exhausting work they had been forced to do and walked right out of the land that had held them in slavery. Right away, God gave them his words, which told them how to live as his free people. They had been set free from slavery to live as God's people. In a similar way, we have been set free from sin—not in order to do whatever we please but in order to serve the one who freed us. How do we do that? By listening to and obeying God's Word and by serving Jesus who paid our debt.

## INTERACTION AND REFLECTION

- Does freedom in Christ mean that Christians can do anything they want?
- What should we do with our newfound freedom?

## 3 FREEDOM TO SERVE OTHERS (20.4)
*Luke 20:19–26*

Have you noticed that in every class there seems to be at least one student who tries to get out of following the rules? If the teacher asks the students to sit up straight in their chairs, this student decides to slouch down. If the principal requests that no student chew bubble gum, then this student comes to school with a brand new pack of gum. Sadly, did you know that what is true of that one student is generally true of us all? Did you notice how the people in our Bible reading today tried to trick Jesus into not submitting to Caesar? They were saying that if we serve God, then we shouldn't have to submit to others who are not following him. Well, Jesus didn't fall for their little trick, and neither should we. Being set free from sin by Christ's death and resurrection doesn't mean that we are free to disobey lesser authorities—far from it. Having been saved from sin, we are free not only to serve God with our whole heart, but also to submit to lesser human authorities too.

## INTERACTION AND REFLECTION

- How do you think we should act and talk about the people who are in charge of us (the authorities over us)?
- Can you recall the five terms the writers of the Confession want us to know about the Bible's teaching on the Christian life? *(Good works, perseverance, assurance, law, and liberty.)*

|||||||||||||||||||||||| *Lesson 21* ||||||||||||||||||||||||

# RELIGIOUS WORSHIP
# AND THE SABBATH DAY

## 1 GOD CARES HOW WE WORSHIP HIM (21.1, 21.3, 21.4, 21.5)
*Genesis 4:1–7*

Jack and Lucas were playing in their bedroom when their father called up from the bottom of the stairs, "Boys, I need each of you to bring me one more clean pair of socks for the suitcase." It was almost Thanksgiving, and Mom and Dad were busy packing the last of the family's clothes for a trip to Grandma's house for the holiday. The boys hollered back in unison, "Sure thing, Dad." Jack went to his dresser and grabbed a clean pair of socks from the drawer. Lucas saw some dirty socks from yesterday still lying on the floor and grabbed those instead. "Hey, you heard what Dad said," said Jack, "Bring a clean pair." "I don't care what Dad said," replied Lucas. "It won't matter."

Do you think the father will be pleased with what both boys bring him? In the same way, our heavenly Father is only pleased when we worship him as he has asked us to. Cain and Abel found that out in our Bible reading today. God uses the story of Cain and Abel to show us how to worship him.

### INTERACTION ⟨AND⟩ REFLECTION

- Do you know what the difference was between Cain and Abel's offering? (*Hebrews 11:4 gives us the answer: faith. Faith is belief in God's Word. Cain must have thought that it didn't matter to God how he worshiped God as long as he brought something.)*

- Can you think of some actions and attitudes that God expects in our worship?

## 2 ONLY CHRISTIAN WORSHIP IS ACCEPTABLE (21.2)
*Revelation 5*

Each year, people who make big-screen movies hand out awards to individuals who do an especially good job. While a number of people are nominated for a particular award, only one lucky person wins. After peeling open the sealed envelope with the winner's name in it, the announcer says, "And the winner is . . ."

Today we read about a different awards ceremony. A sealed scroll needed to be opened, but it held bigger news than a winner from a movie. This scroll, once opened, would let loose seven specific acts of God's judgment against the world for sin. This scroll couldn't be opened by just anyone—it had to be opened by someone who could rightly unleash God's judgment on an unbelieving world. At first it looked like no one was worthy for such an assignment—until the Lamb of God, Jesus, stepped forward. He alone is worthy to carry out God's will. Not you. Not me. Not any other living person. Not angels or even godly people who died long, long ago.

Since Jesus is the only person who is worthy, he is the only one we are to worship. God will not accept worship that comes to him in just any name. Prayers and praises that are offered in Jesus's name are the only ones God will hear.

So far in this lesson, we've learned two important things about worship. First, God cares how we worship him: we are to worship him in faith. Second, God has told us how we come to him in faith: through faith in Jesus Christ, the Lamb of God, who alone is worthy.

## INTERACTION *AND* REFLECTION

- Who is the only person worthy of receiving our praise and worship?
- Why do people who believe the Bible end their prayers by saying, "I ask this in Jesus's name"?

## 3 GOD'S WEEKLY GIFT (21.7, 21.8)
*Psalm 84*

Do you ever trade food in your lunch for something you like better that someone else has brought? Isn't it fun to trade with other kids? Maybe you trade your carrots for someone's apple or a handful of gummy bears for a peanut butter cup. In this lesson we have been learning about worship, and we just read that the psalmist would gladly trade a thousand days of being anywhere in the world for a single day spent in the presence of God! That is how much he wanted to spend time with God. Did you know that God has already given you one day out of every seven to spend entirely with him? Sunday is the Lord's Day. It is the day we should worship God and put other things away. Since God has given us this day as a gift, we should use it to worship him and focus on what he has done for us.

## INTERACTION *AND* REFLECTION

- What are some of the sad things we trade worship for on Sunday?
- What do you think would happen if every Christian took their Sunday worship seriously?

# ||||||||||||||||||| *Lesson 22* |||||||||||||||||||

# LAWFUL OATHS AND VOWS

## 1 THERE ARE OCCASIONS FOR OATHS AND VOWS (22.1, 22.2, 22.3)
*Ecclesiastes 5:1–7*

Have you ever had this experience: suddenly a great idea jumps into your mind about doing something nice for someone you love? Perhaps you want to write him a card or paint a picture just for her. The same thing happens after spending time with God. Suddenly, we find ourselves wanting to do something especially for him . . . or we find that our minds are filled with something that we feel he really wants us to do.

Our Bible reading today teaches us that while there will be times we feel like this, we should only promise to do it after really thinking through the commitment. God is happy when we promise to do something for him. That promise is called a vow. But be careful! Don't make promises on the strength of your own name, or the name of earth, or even heaven. Make them by the name of God alone, for he alone is able to help you fulfill them (Deut. 10:20; Matt. 5:33–34). Make sure that before you promise to do something in God's name, you are sure, in faith, that God wants you to do it. Don't take your promises to God lightly.

## INTERACTION ⟨AND⟩ REFLECTION

- In this lesson the writers of the Confession want us to see the importance of keeping our word. Why is this so essential to our Christian life?

- Do you think all people think that keeping their word is important? What are some ways that people show they don't value keeping their word?

## 2 GUARD YOUR VOWS (22.3, 22.4)
*Acts 18:18*

Why do you think we read this verse today? Perhaps you are scratching your head about why it's an important verse. Normally, we don't read just one verse without much context. But this verse does have something to teach us about making vows. The apostle Paul made a vow. He cut his hair as a sign of what he promised before God. Paul was keeping his word. You and I need to learn to be promise keepers too. If your word is not good, then people won't be able to trust much of what you say. Keeping our promises to God is one of the most important things we can do to help people to understand that our God is a promise-keeping God.

### INTERACTION ⟡AND⟡ REFLECTION

- Do you think it is wise to makes lots of promises to people? Why or why not?
- Why do you think we have such a problem keeping our word? Does God?

## 3 KEEP YOUR VOWS (22.5, 22.6, 22.7)
*Psalm 15*

Summer was coming, and Ben really wanted to go to camp with his friends. His parents told him that he could go if he kept his room clean for a month—his bed made each morning and everything! Ben promised to do just that. A few days later, Ben was playing with 143 matchbox racecars all over his bedroom floor. The phone rang. Ben's friend was calling from his mom's cell phone. "Hi, Ben, we are in a big hurry, but I wondered if you wanted to come with us to get ice cream. Can you be ready in one minute?" Boy, did Ben want to go! But he also knew he would have to clean up his 143 cars and there wasn't time to do both. "Thanks, but I can't come this time," said Ben. "I've got other commitments that I already made." Ben kept his word to his parents, and later that summer he received his reward.

The psalmist today told us who gets the reward of dwelling with God. It is the one who speaks truthfully (v. 2) even when keeping his promise means missing out on things (v. 4). Be a person who keeps your commitments to God in Christ. One day you will get your reward!

## INTERACTION ⟨AND⟩ REFLECTION

- Can you think of a time when keeping your word was hard?
- How important is God's promise of dwelling with him to you? Is that promise a good motivator to keep your word now?

IIIIIIIIIIIIIIIIIIII *Lesson 23* IIIIIIIIIIIIIIIIIIII

# THE CIVIL AUTHORITIES

## 1 ESTABLISHED BY GOD (23.1)
*Romans 13:1–7*

Tyrone and Jasmine were arguing over the remote control for the television. Taylor, their babysitter, heard them from the next room. She came into the room and said, "I'm sorry, guys, but you will have to turn the TV off now and find something else to do." "Do we really have to?" the children asked. "Yes," replied Taylor. "Your parents left me in charge, and they told me that if you argued over the TV you would have to turn it off." Tyrone and Jasmine obeyed the babysitter right away.

Babysitters don't always have an easy job. They have the unique but challenging task of watching *over* children while serving *under* parents. We can look at authorities in government in the same way. They don't have an easy job. But God established their role for the good of all people. Government is charged by God to serve *over* people and *under* God. You and I should live under the government in a way that pleases God. We should also pray for those whom God has put in authority over us (1 Tim. 2:1–4), so that they will govern us according to God's righteous and just rule.

## INTERACTION ⟨AND⟩ REFLECTION

- In this lesson we will be learning about another aspect of Christian life: our relationship to human government. Can you tell me any of the jobs that people fill in the government? Can you tell me any of the names of people who are in government over us? *(Hint: They could be in charge of your city, or state, or country.)*

- God asks us to pray for the people in government who serve over us. Take a minute to do that now.

# 2 A NOBLE CALLING (23.2, 23.3)
*Daniel 2:1, 16–24, 46–49*

Have you ever put together a jigsaw puzzle? Imagine almost completing a puzzle only to find out at the end that some pieces are missing! That would be frustrating, wouldn't it? I don't want you to be frustrated by our Bible reading today, so let me fill in the missing pieces. King Neb had a dream. He dreamed about a giant statue that looked like a mighty king. Its head was made of gold, its middle and thighs were made of bronze, and its feet were made partly of iron and partly of clay. There was only one problem—King Neb didn't know what the dream meant. Then God showed Daniel the dream and what it meant. Daniel told the king that God was the one who removes kings and sets them up in authority. He told King Neb that he was the head of the statue, but that after him would come other kingdoms . . . until God set up his own kingdom that would never end. This made the king very happy, and he put Daniel and his three friends in charge of his government. What a good thing for the people of that day to have God-fearing men like Daniel and his friends working in government. What a good thing for us when Christians today serve God in this way too.

## INTERACTION AND REFLECTION

- In a republic like the United States, anyone, regardless of his or her religious beliefs, can serve in government. When Christians work in government, how can they use their jobs to serve the Lord and the people in this country?
- Why might it be good for a Christian to be in government?

## 3 THE PURPOSE TO WHICH ALL HISTORY AND GOVERNMENT IS MOVING (23.1)
*Psalm 2*

Tug of war is a fun game to play with lots of people. Are you familiar with it? Two teams each grab the end of a rope and try with all their strength to pull the other team across the middle point. It is a test to see who is stronger. In our Bible reading today, we saw what turned out to be a humorous tug of war. The nations were on one side of the rope, trying to govern the world for their own glory; they pulled with all their strength in an effort to overthrow God and his king. Yet God was on the other side of the rope, laughing at their insufficient efforts. He had set up Jesus as his supreme ruler. He established Jesus's authority. Therefore, every human authority, every nation, every ruler and king, would do well to live under the rule of Jesus, unless they want to be punished later.

## INTERACTION AND REFLECTION

- In our Bible reading today, we learned that human governments are not the final authority in human history. Think about the American War for Independence or perhaps another war you've studied at school. How does knowing that God is the final authority change your understanding of that war?
- What can Christians do to help government leaders understand that their role is to serve under God?

# ||||||||||||||||||| Lesson 24 |||||||||||||||||||

# MARRIAGE AND DIVORCE

## 1 ONE MAN AND ONE WOMAN IN THE LORD (24.1, 24.3)
*Mark 10:1–9*

Think about a time when you had to take a test. Tests help teachers to measure what we know about a subject. Every teacher wants his or her students to do well on a test. Imagine taking a test for a teacher who wanted you to fail! Wouldn't that be terrible? Yet that is precisely what happened to Jesus. The Bible teachers, known as the Pharisees, gave him a test on marriage, and they were hoping he would fail. They thought that if they could trick Jesus into disagreeing with the great teacher Moses, perhaps the crowds would stop listening to him and pay attention to them again. Jesus didn't fail their evil test! His answer teaches us three important things about marriage. First, when God created people, he created us male and female; when God made you a boy or girl, he knew exactly what he was doing. Second, from the beginning, it was God's plan that men would marry women and women would marry men. It was never God's intention for men to marry men, or women to marry women. Third, whenever a man takes a woman to be his wife, their marriage should be for life; we should be very careful to do all we can to not separate what God joined together.

## INTERACTION AND REFLECTION

- This lesson on marriage is the last of the Confession's lessons on the Christian life. Can you recall the other seven topics? (*Good works, perseverance, assurance, law, liberty, oaths, and government.*)

Can you tell me the three things we learned today that teach us that marriage should be reserved for one man and one woman? *(1. When God created man he made them male and female. 2. God intended for only men and women to be joined in marriage. 3. What God intended to be joined, a male and female, he does not want to be separated. This is how Jesus interprets the Hebrew Scriptures [see Matt. 19].)*

## 2 A BLESSED GIFT (24.2)
*Psalm 128*

I can promise you one thing for sure: when you grow up, your life will get really busy! Do you know what happens to grown-ups who get too busy? Sometimes they forget things or take people for granted. The psalm that we just read is a great reminder for married people who are too busy. It teaches them what is really important in life: having God's blessing. We learn that a man who has a wife and children is greatly blessed. After we read about this man's wife and children in verse 3, it says in the next verse, "*Thus* shall the man be blessed." Marriage is a huge blessing, a great gift! When God gives a man a wife, he has given him a relationship to be envied. And when God gives a woman a husband, she is also given a huge blessing. Now, this doesn't mean that every Christian must have a spouse and children to be blessed by God. But those who do should slow down and count their special blessings! Marriage is a gift, and we ought to help those who are married to treasure their marriage with their whole heart.

## INTERACTION ⟨AND⟩ REFLECTION

- Why do you think the Bible says marriage is a gift from God? Name some reasons.
- Think about someone you know who is married. Can you say or do something for them that might remind them how blessed they are to be married?

## 3 THE TRAGEDY OF UNFAITHFULNESS (24.5, 24.6)
*Proverbs 6:20–35*

Liza yelled, "Ready or not, here I come!" as she pulled her hands away from her eyes. Then she raced off in one direction after another looking for her friends who were hiding. Do you enjoy playing hide and seek? It's fun, isn't it? Can you tell me why the person who is "it" yells, "Ready or not, here I come!!" Those words warn the others that the game has begun—and they'd better be ready!

Our Bible reading today functions in a similar way. God is yelling to us, "OK, I have given you a fair warning! You had better be ready to listen to my words!" God's voice is calling out to men and warning them about only having one woman for a wife. If you are a young boy or girl, I hope you listen to these words. Be very careful how you treat people. Respect them. Respect your own body too. Marriage is a holy relationship and should be kept pure. If we are not married to someone, we must not treat them in the special way that we are to treat only our husband or wife. And remember: God can see us, God called out to us, and one day God will seek us out whether we are ready or not.

## INTERACTION AND REFLECTION

- Do you normally think of a warning as a good thing or a bad thing? Why, or why not?
- Why do you think King David taught Solomon about marriage when he was just a young boy (see Proverbs 4)? Does hearing the Word as a kid mean you will follow it as an adult? What steps can you take to be a follower of God's Word?

# Part Six

# The
# Church

IIIIIIIIIIIIIIIIIIIIIIIII *Lesson* 25 IIIIIIIIIIIIIIIIIIIIIIII

# THE CHURCH

## 1 ONE BODY, ONE HEAD (25.1, 25.2)
*1 Peter 2:1–10*

If you were asked to describe "the church," what words would you use? The Bible uses the image of a body to describe the church. We are part of the same body, and Jesus is the head of the body. Christians are people who trust in Jesus alone for salvation, and Christians make up the church's body. We belong to one body of believers around the world and throughout history. We belong to the same body as Perpetua, a woman who was martyred for her faith in North Africa in the year AD 203; the same body as the Roman emperor Constantine, who became a Christian around the year 337 and forever changed the course of history; the same body as Johann Sebastian Bach, a German musician who composed countless pieces of beautiful music for the glory of God; the same body as Pentecostal Christians in South Korea; the same body as Catholic Christians in Poland; and the same body as Christians in parts of the world who today are persecuted for their faith. We belong to the same body, and serve the same Lord, Jesus Christ.

### INTERACTION ⟨AND⟩ REFLECTION

- In this lesson we begin Part 6 of *Big Beliefs!* Try to recall the first five parts. *(God's Word; God; The Fall, Sin, and Mankind; Salvation; and The Christian Life.)*

- Can you name some other people, past or present, around the world or across the street, who are part of this body known as the church?

## 2 THE FAMILY OF GOD (25.2)
*Psalm 87*

In addition to the image of the human body, the Bible uses the image of a family to describe the church. God is our Father, and other Christians are our brothers and sisters. Have you ever thought, "What is it that makes me part of my family?" There are actually two ways that someone can become part of a family. One way is to be born into a family, and the other is to be adopted into a family. Either way, you are just as much a part of your family whether you were born or adopted into it. Do you know how we become part of God's family? The Bible tells us that when it comes to God's family, we are born ("born again") *and* adopted into it. In this way, God's family is unlike any other. It's as if God wants our relationship to his family to be twice as strong as our regular family. So whether we were born or adopted into our regular family, each of us can also say that we have been born into a family *and* adopted into a family—God's family.

### INTERACTION AND REFLECTION

- So far we have learned two ways that the Bible speaks of the church. What are they? *(The church is called a body and a family.)*
- How did you become part of your family? How do we become part of God's family?

## 3 THE WAY OF GRACE (25.3)
*2 Chronicles 6:40–7:3*

Imagine that you are on an island full of people. A disease on the island has infected everyone, and there is no medicine on the island to cure them. The only way to find a cure is to leave the island and travel to a place with the right medicine. There are no airplanes, but a ship large enough for everyone is willing to take people to receive medical help. Would you climb aboard? Or would you look for another way to get off the island?

Several lessons ago, when we talked about God's covenant with mankind (lesson 7), we compared the church to a journey toward a final destination, and the final destination to God's grace in Jesus Christ. Likewise, in the illustration of the boat and the island, the boat is like the church. The church is the way that God has chosen to bring sinners into fellowship with each other and into stronger relationship with him. It is God's way of providing grace to everyone who is in his Son, Jesus Christ. Our Bible passage today from the Old Testament described the glory of the Lord filling the temple. Jesus Christ was God in the flesh, and the church is his body (his physical presence in the world), and that means that the glory of the Lord lives in the church.

## INTERACTION AND REFLECTION

- An old church father named Augustine of Hippo once said that there is no salvation outside the church. What do you think he meant by this?
- Why is the church the only "ship" that can take us to safety?

IIIIIIIIIIIIIIIIIIIII *Lesson 26* IIIIIIIIIIIIIIIIIIIII

# THE COMMUNION OF SAINTS

## 1 UNITED WITH CHRIST (26.1)
*Hebrews 2:10–18*

Have you ever visited the White House in Washington, DC? That is where the president of the United States and his family live. If you plan carefully, you can take a tour of part of the White House with other visitors. There are many places in the building where visitors are not allowed. But what if you knew the president personally? You might be invited to visit the White House, and you could see the parts that ordinary visitors are not allowed to see. The president could just say, "They're with me," and you could go wherever the president took you. As Christians who are part of the church, you and I are part of the "communion of saints." This means that we have access to everything that Jesus Christ has provided for us, because we are united with him. When Jesus says, "They're with me," that is far more wonderful than being friends with the president.

## INTERACTION ⟨AND⟩ REFLECTION

- In the last lesson we learned *what* the church is called (body and family) as well as its importance. In this lesson we learn *who* the church is. It's not the building where we meet, is it? Who makes up the church?
- Why is it really wonderful to be united with Jesus? What kinds of things does Jesus provide you with?

## 2 UNITED WITH ONE ANOTHER (26.1)
*Psalm 133*

Have you heard of the World Wide Web? It is abbreviated WWW, and if you use a computer to use the Internet, you are on the World Wide Web. It is a way for people all over the world to communicate and exchange information with each other with the click of a button. The World Wide Web has changed the way people live and work in ways that no one could have imagined. But the idea of a worldwide community of people is not new; it was what God had in mind ever since he created his family, what we now call the church. The church is a "communion of saints," and that means that all Christians are part of the same family and the same body. As part of the communion of saints, we care about other Christians' sorrow, pain, happiness, and success, and we share our love and devotion to our one Lord, Jesus Christ.

## INTERACTION ⟨AND⟩ REFLECTION

- Can you think of someone in the communion of saints who may need encouragement or help? What practical thing can you do this week to encourage that person?
- In what ways could you use the World Wide Web to communicate with Christians around the world? How do you see people doing this already?

## 3 FOR THE GOOD OF THE BODY (26.2)
*Exodus 35:20–29*

You probably don't think about it very often, but each and every part of your body plays an important role in the health and operation of your whole body. Most of your body parts work without your even thinking about them, even when you are sleeping. When a part of your body is sick or injured, you realize just how much you need it. In this lesson and the one before, we have talked about the church and the communion of saints as a body and as a family. In the communion of saints, that is, the church, each person is an important part of the body, no matter if he or she is an elderly person, an infant, a single parent, a teenager, or someone with a disability. Every Christian plays an important role in the family and has something to contribute to the health and benefit of the other members. This means that we should appreciate our own part in the body of Christ, but it also means that we should appreciate the part others play in the body.

## INTERACTION ⟨AND⟩ REFLECTION

- Who are some people in the church that you are thankful for? Why are you thankful for them?
- Why do some parts of the body get more attention than others? Is that wrong? Why, or why not?

# THE SACRAMENTS

## 1 CHRIST AND HIS BENEFITS (27.1, 27.4)
*1 Corinthians 10:1–6*

*Sacrament.* That is a big word, a word you may not hear very often. A sacrament is an action that God has given to the church in order to give us his grace. The way that God provides grace to us is through his Son, Jesus Christ. Jesus has died for our sins, rose again, and ascended into heaven, where he intercedes for us as our priest. By doing these things, Jesus has secured many benefits for us, including adoption into God's family, forgiveness of our sins, our growth in Christ-likeness, and the promise of eternal life. There are two sacraments that Jesus commanded in the New Testament: baptism and the Lord's Supper. We will talk more about them in the coming lessons. Our passage for today is important because it uses the language of baptism and the Lord's Supper ("eating and drinking") to show us that we, like the Israelites long ago, truly receive God's grace through Jesus in the sacraments.

## INTERACTION AND REFLECTION

- The writers of the Confession want us to see a third important truth from the Bible about the church. The church has been given two sacraments. What are these two sacraments? Can you explain what a sacrament is?
- Because of God's grace given to us through Jesus Christ, what are some of the benefits you receive?

# 2 MORE THAN MEETS THE EYE (27.2)
*Psalm 105:37–45*

Jeremiah receives letters from his grandmother, and at the end of each letter, she writes OXOXOX. Do you know what that means? The O's are hugs, and the X's are kisses. This is a signal that tells Jeremiah that his grandmother is hugging and kissing him, even though he cannot see her. The word *sacrament* literally means "mystery." This word was used to describe baptism and the Lord's Supper because, in those actions, God—who is invisible—is doing things that cannot be seen by the eye. People therefore called these actions a "mystery," or a sacrament. Today's passage from Psalm 105 talks about the Israelites' journey through the wilderness, including when they drank water from a rock. They did not realize it at the time, but they were drinking from a spiritual Rock, Jesus. (The apostle Paul talks about this in the passage we read yesterday from 1 Corinthians.) In baptism and the Lord's Supper, God uses regular things—like water, bread, wine, and the words and actions of the pastor performing the sacrament—as signals that he is doing wonderful things that we cannot see with our physical eyes.

## INTERACTION AND REFLECTION

- What are some other signals in everyday life that indicate something bigger is happening that we cannot see? *(Railroad crossing gates signal a train is approaching, a mom's pregnant belly means a baby is coming, the sounds of an ice cream truck announce ice cream is on its way!)*
- How should we treat the sacraments of baptism and the Lord's Supper knowing that God is at work in them? *(Reverence, self-examination, thankfulness, joy.)*

# 3 THE HOLY SPIRIT AT WORK (27.3)
*John 3:1–8*

Many people today think that unless something can be explained by natural events or by science, it cannot be true. When God does his work in the sacraments, it cannot be explained naturally, because it is not a natural thing—we say that it is *supernatural*. When you take a bath or shower, the water and soap wash away the dirt and make your body clean. This is what water naturally does. When we are baptized, the Holy Spirit does something with the water that an ordinary bath does not do. It is supernatural. When you eat a meal, the food and drink strengthen your body and make you grow. This is what food and drink naturally do. When we eat and drink at the Lord's Supper, the Holy Spirit does things in us that ordinary food and drink cannot do. In the next two lessons, we will take a closer look at these two sacraments, baptism and the Lord's Supper.

## INTERACTION AND REFLECTION

- Name some other things that God has done, in the Bible or not, that are supernatural.
- In this lesson we have concentrated on the sacraments. The next two lessons will look at the sacraments of baptism and the Lord's Supper individually. Take a minute to thank God for these sacraments.

# BAPTISM

## 1 ENTRY INTO THE FAMILY (28.1, 28.2, 28.4, 28.7)
*Matthew 28:16–20*

A few lessons ago we talked about how a person becomes part of a family. Do you remember the two ways we discussed? One way is by being born into a family; the other is through adoption. When it comes to God's family, the church, we are born *and* adopted into it. We cannot see what it looks like to be born again and adopted into God's family, so God gave us the sacrament of baptism to be an outward sign of our entry into his family. In our Scripture passage today, we read the last words that Jesus spoke to his disciples before he ascended into heaven. This passage is often called the "Great Commission." Jesus told his disciples to go and make other disciples. *Disciple* is another name for a Christian—a member of God's family. Jesus told his disciples to make other disciples by baptizing them in the name of the Father, and of the Son, and of the Holy Spirit, and by teaching them to do everything Jesus commanded. So we see from this passage that baptism is the first part of becoming a disciple—it signifies that we are a member of God's family.

### INTERACTION AND REFLECTION

- According to the words of Jesus, would you say that baptism is an important part of following Jesus?
- After baptism, what is the second part of becoming a disciple, according to our passage?

## 2 ALL OF CHRIST'S BENEFITS (28.1, 28.4, 28.6)
*Colossians 2:8–15*

In the children's story *The Voyage of the Dawn Treader*, author C. S. Lewis describes a very special picture that some children discovered one day. The picture was hanging on the wall, and it showed a beautiful scene that attracted the children to it. But this was no ordinary picture. When the children drew near and touched it, they actually *entered into* the scene of the picture. They had crossed into another world! Baptism can be compared to this special picture. Baptism is a sign that we are part of God's family, and therefore we are united to Christ. It is beautiful to behold. But as long as you only look at the picture, you do not experience these blessings. Baptism is more than a picture; it is like the special picture in the story—those who are baptized show that through faith they have entered into God's family picture and receive all the blessings that God has provided for his children through the life, death, resurrection, and ascension of his Son. It is a picture that you and I become part of when we are baptized.

### INTERACTION ⟨AND⟩ REFLECTION

- Can you name some of the benefits that God has provided us through Christ his Son?
- What do you think the apostle Paul means in our Bible reading today when he says that we have been "buried with [Jesus] in baptism" (v. 12)?

## 3 A NEW WAY OF LIFE (28.1, 28.6)
*Titus 3:1–11*

What does it mean when someone says something was a turning point in his or her life? Not only does baptism introduce us into the family of God, and not only does it give us access to every blessing that Jesus has provided for us, but baptism also marks a turning point in our lives. As baptized members of God's family, we have the responsibilities of being in God's family. What kind of responsibilities do you have as part of your family? Do you wash dishes, take out the garbage, or clean your room? As a family member, you have the responsibility of honoring and obeying your parents and getting along with your siblings. And because you have your family's last name, you also have the responsibility of behaving well in public and in private, because anything that you do, good or bad, will be reflected on your entire family. As baptized Christians, we have the incredible honor of representing God's name, and it is a great privilege to glorify him in our thoughts, words, and deeds.

## INTERACTION AND REFLECTION

- We have seen both the benefits and responsibilities of baptism. If you have been baptized, what are your new responsibilities as a follower of Jesus?
- The Holy Spirit helps us to honor and obey God, but sometimes we dishonor and disobey him and need to ask for God's forgiveness. Ask God to forgive you, and then ask the Holy Spirit to help you to fulfill your responsibilities in God's family.

# ||||||||||||||||||| *Lesson 29* |||||||||||||||||||

# THE LORD'S SUPPER

## 1 CHRIST'S BODY AND BLOOD (29.1, 29.3, 29.5–8)
*John 6:22–35*

Have you ever heard someone say, "You are what you eat"? What does that mean? Does it mean that you will become a hamburger, or a carrot, or a jelly bean? No, what it means is that if you eat healthy food, you will be healthy and strong, but if you eat sweets and junk food, you will not. But what does this mean for the bread and wine that represent Jesus's body and blood in the Lord's Supper? Jesus himself gave us an answer in our passage today in John 6. When he said these things, Jesus had not yet introduced the Lord's Supper to his disciples; however, the people who heard John's gospel after Jesus ascended to heaven would certainly have thought of the Lord's Supper. Jesus tells the people that he is like the manna that God gave to the Israelites to keep them alive—give them life—in the desert. Jesus says *he* is the Bread of Life, and that if we come to him we will not hunger or thirst. The Lord's Supper reminds us where we get the things necessary for eternal life—from Jesus, and his death and resurrection. Eating and drinking the bread and wine of the Lord's Supper strengthens us in our union with Christ.

## INTERACTION *AND* REFLECTION

- In this lesson the writers of the Confession have us focus on the sacrament of the Lord's Supper. According to our Bible reading today, what does Jesus call himself? How is Jesus like the manna given to the Israelites?

- What do you think Jesus means when he says we will never be hungry if we believe in him?

## 2 A DIVINE MEMORIAL (29.1)
*1 Corinthians 11:23–26*

Do you know what a memorial is? A memorial is a reminder—it brings back the memory of a great event or an important person. Oftentimes, people set up memorials in the form of large monuments, like sculptures and statues, or they might perform special ceremonies. In Washington, DC, there are several memorials. One of the most famous is the Lincoln Memorial. It is dedicated to the sixteenth president of the United States, Abraham Lincoln. Everyone who sees it is reminded of what he did. Did you know that God likes to be reminded as well? Of course, this does not mean that God ever forgets—in fact, he cannot forget. But he likes to be reminded of his unforgettable work of grace in giving Jesus Christ as the sacrifice for our sins on the cross. The Lord's Supper is a memorial. It serves to remind us of Jesus's ultimate love for his people, the church. It also serves to remind God of his promise to forgive our sins because of what Jesus did.

## INTERACTION AND REFLECTION

- When you remember what Jesus did for you on the cross, is this a sad or a happy memory? Why did you choose the answer you did?
- Why do you think Jesus gave us the Lord's Supper as a memorial? (Note: *Talk to your kids about the benefits of reminders in other areas of life.*)

# 3 A NOURISHING FEAST (29.1, 29.7)
## *Psalm 34:1–10*

Can you name some foods that not only taste good but also are good for you? Of course, everyone's taste is not the same. Some people like broccoli, which is very good for you, but other people don't like the taste of broccoli. Many people like ice cream and cookies, but they are not good for you, especially if you eat them all the time. What about the bread and wine of the Lord's Supper? In this meal we eat just a small piece of bread and drink just a little wine or grape juice, and so the taste and the physical health value are not considered very important. What can we say about the "supernatural" value of the meal? We have already talked about how important this sacrament is for our spiritual health. Psalm 34:8 says, "Taste and see that the LORD is good." Indeed, the Lord's Supper is a meal that not only nourishes your soul but is also good for you!

## INTERACTION AND REFLECTION

- We have been in Part 6 of *Big Beliefs!* for five lessons. Part 6 teaches us wonderful things related to the church. In this lesson, what did we learn about the Lord's Supper?
- Can you think of some ways that the Lord's Supper strengthens us spiritually? *(As a picture of Jesus's body and blood, it focuses our eyes on Jesus, the Bread of Life, and strengthens our union with him. As a memorial, it reminds us what Jesus has done for us and helps us to persevere in our Christian life.)*

|||||||||||||||||||||| *Lesson 30* ||||||||||||||||||||||

# CHURCH DISCIPLINE

## 1 GODLY LEADERSHIP (30.1, 30.2, 30.3)
*Isaiah 9:6–7*

In the city of Chicago, police cars have a symbol painted on the side with the words *We serve and protect.* Those words remind everyone of the two primary roles a police officer fulfills. Officers have the special privilege of serving the community and protecting its citizens from danger and harm. Chicago is fortunate to have a host of officers who serve and protect. Their job is not easy. At times, they have to do difficult things to maintain peace and order in the community.

In the church, God has set up the roles of church officers, known as elders, who are charged to serve and protect people in the community of faith. One of the ways they serve and protect us is through something called a *censure.* A censure is a warning or command given to people who are straying away from Jesus. For example, if someone in the church is telling lies or saying mean things, the elders in their role as protectors will warn, or censure, that person not to harm other members. A censure is a good thing given to the church by God to maintain peace and purity in Christ's family. It is one of the ways Jesus upholds his government with justice and righteousness.

### INTERACTION 〈AND〉 REFLECTION

- In this lesson we are learning about the importance and benefits of discipline in the church. Why do you think God wants us to have church officers? Why is it important to have censures?

- Take a few minutes to pray for your church leaders, asking God to help them serve and protect the church of Jesus Christ.

## 2 A CHARGE TO ELDERS (30.1)
*1 Peter 5:1–4*

There is a saying that goes like this: "At the end of the day, everyone has to answer to someone." Can you tell me what this saying might mean? In a simple way, I guess we could say that it means all people—no matter how many people they have under their authority—still have someone that is over them, someone to whom they are personally accountable. In our Bible reading today, Peter reminds the elders of this very idea. He wants the elders of the church to know that the church is not their own. They are under-shepherds for the chief Shepherd, Jesus. This truth helps the men who are in authority in the church apply their leadership carefully. They themselves are under the authority of Jesus. This truth is a wonderful help to elders because it makes them carry out the tough job of leadership, and at times disciplining, with humility and strength.

### INTERACTION AND REFLECTION

- How should we pray for the elders in our church?
- Are you glad that God has set up elders in the church to help shepherd you? Whom else has he put in authority over you?

## 3 AS A FATHER LOVES HIS CHILDREN (30.3, 30.4)
*Psalm 32*

Little Nathan stood in the doorway screaming, "No! No! I'm not coming inside for my bath no matter what you say!" Nathan's dad tried to get him to settle down, even offering him candy if he would please come inside. Nathan didn't move. Eventually his dad said, "All right, Nathan, you win. You don't have to take a bath tonight." Now, can you imagine what kind of man Nathan might grow up to be like? Worse yet, can you imagine having a father who knows that you need a bath but allows you not to take one? Today in our world, fathers often think that they are loving their children by letting them do whatever they please. Fortunately, God does not act like this kind of father. He loves us *too much*. While God forgives us of our sins, he still disciplines us for our good. After David sinned against God, he prayed for forgiveness and God forgave him. But God punished him too. Disobedient behavior needs correcting, and God has given his church censures to admonish and correct disobedient people. Never think that censures in the church are unloving or too harsh. Censures are given to disobedient Christians who refuse to repent, but the goal and hope of a censure is always that the person will repent and be restored to the church. A loving father disciplines those he loves, and leaders in the church are to act like God in this way.

## INTERACTION AND REFLECTION

- Do you think that discipline is a good thing or a bad thing? Why?
- God loves his children too much to let them do whatever they please. Should we be angry or thankful that God gives us leaders who will discipline us when we speak or act sinfully?

|||||||||||||||||||||| *Lesson 31* ||||||||||||||||||||||

# SYNODS AND COUNCILS

## 1 FOR THE CHURCH'S GOOD (31.1, 31.2)
*Acts 15:22–35*

Do you like going to the library to check out books? Did you know that every library has a special section of books called *reference works*? These books—dictionaries, thesauruses, almanacs, and catalogs, for example—help us when we are trying to find an answer to a perplexing problem. Did you know that God gave the church something like a reference library? He did, but instead of a reference library, God gave his church gatherings of godly people called synods and councils. One such council was mentioned in our Bible reading today. When the church has trouble answering a perplexing question, many learned and godly people assemble to talk about it. This has happened numerous times throughout the history of the church. When the church was trying to answer the perplexing question of whether or not Jesus is fully God and fully man, they called a council meeting. The same thing happened when the church was trying to understand the Trinity. Isn't it great to know that you have these rich resources of synods and councils to help guide you?

## INTERACTION ⟨AND⟩ REFLECTION

- This lesson marks the end of Part 6 on the church. Can you recall the seven headings? *(The church; the communion of saints; the sacraments; baptism; the Lord's Supper; church discipline; and this lesson, synods and councils.)*

- Check out a dictionary of the church from the library or go online to see if you can find out any information on church councils and what they were about.

## 2 WISDOM FOR FAITH AND PRACTICE (31.1)
*Proverbs 1:1–7*

Rabbits are known for eating carrots. Horses are known for galloping very fast. And dogs are known for being man's best friend. What are owls known for? The answer is wisdom, as described in this nursery rhyme:

A wise old owl lived in an oak
The more he saw the less he spoke
The less he spoke the more he heard.
Why can't we all be like that wise old bird?

After listening to the Bible reading today, I guess you could say that, if you were an animal, you would want to be an owl! Proverbs tells us repeatedly that we ought to work hard at getting wisdom. We can get wisdom in a number of ways, but the first way is clear: "The fear of the LORD is the beginning of knowledge; fools despise wisdom and instruction" (v. 7). Growing up to be a wise person will mean paying close attention to God's Word. It also means listening to the wisdom that is passed down to you by older people. Did you know that if you study the church councils and synods, you will find much wisdom there, too? The teaching passed down to us from these councils is the fruit of many "wise old owls" who worked hard at understanding God's Word.

## INTERACTION AND REFLECTION
- Why do you think that listening to the wisdom that is passed down to you is important for becoming a wise person?

- Proverbs says that the first step to become wise is "the fear of the LORD." This doesn't mean God is scary; it means we should give all honor to God and that we should love and obey no other gods but him. Why do you think this kind of fear will make you wise?

## 3 AGREEMENT WITH THE SCRIPTURES (31.3)
*Psalm 119:1–8*

Can you tell me what fruit the state of Florida is famous for? Florida is known for its oranges! Few breakfast drinks are more refreshing than a tall glass of cold orange juice, especially when the label on the carton reads: "100% pure orange juice." While we have benefited from church councils and synods, remember that only the Bible is "100% pure." God's Word is true in every respect. It is never wrong. Human councils throughout history are helpful, but remember: they are not holy. They are not equal to God's Word. Church councils can help us to learn the truth only if they agree with Scripture and help us to understand it better. If you keep studying God's Word, you will be refreshed and strong—fit to live a life of wisdom and grace.

### INTERACTION *AND* REFLECTION

- If the Bible alone is completely true, pure, and authoritative, is there any value in learning about things outside the Bible, like mathematics, science, and grammar?
- Thank God for the many people in history who wrestled with the meaning of the Bible in ways that help us to become wise.

# Part Seven

# The Last Things

# |||||||||||||||||||||| *Lesson 32* ||||||||||||||||||||||

# THE STATE OF MEN AFTER DEATH AND THE RESURRECTION OF THE DEAD

## 1 PRESENT WITH THE LORD (32.1)
*Luke 23:26–27, 32–33, 39–43*

It's interesting to read the last words of famous people right before they died. When a famous person dies, everyone is interested in knowing what their last words were. For instance, Queen Elizabeth I's last words were, "To have lived and loved and triumphed; and now to know it is over! One may defy everything but this." The last words General William Booth, founder of the Salvation Army, spoke in public were, "While there remains one dark soul without the light of God, I'll fight—I'll fight—I'll fight to the very end." The final words of John Wesley the preacher were, "The best of all is, God is with us." Someone's last words may be interesting, but our Bible reading today gives us even greater words to remember! In his final hours, Jesus spoke to one of the thieves hanging on the cross next to him. He said, "Truly, I say to you, today you will be with me in Paradise" (v. 43). In those words we learn a happy truth: when death comes to those who love Jesus, their souls immediately go to be with him in the presence of God! If Jesus knows us, we don't need to fear death. Now those are great words!

## INTERACTION ⟨AND⟩ REFLECTION

- Wow, we have reached the last part of the Confession! Part 7 is about things that take place at the end of our lives and the end of the world. Let's see if we can remember the seven parts of *Big Beliefs!* (*God's Word; God; The Fall, Sin, and Mankind; Salvation; The Christian Life; The Church; and, finally, The Last Things.*)
- When Christians die, their souls go immediately to be with God in heaven. How does this truth strengthen your love for God?

## 2 TWO DESTINIES (32.3)
*Psalm 1*

J. R. R. Tolkien's *The Hobbit* unfolds the exciting adventures of a delightful character named Bilbo Baggins. After a long time away, Bilbo is nearing home. Tolkien writes,

> Coming to a rise he could see his own Hill in the distance, and he stopped suddenly and said:
>
> . . . Roads go ever ever on
>    Under cloud and under star.
> Yet feet that wandering have gone
>    Turn at last to home afar.
> Eyes that fire and sword have seen
>    And horror in the halls of stone
> Look at last on meadows green,
>    And trees and hills they long have known.[1]

---

1. J. R. R. Tolkien, *The Hobbit* (Boston: Houghton Mifflin, 1966), 313.

Psalm 1 teaches us that after our own adventures in this life, we too will turn at last toward home. Once we die, we will stand before the God who made us and look on his greatness. Each of us will give an account for how we lived. For those who love Jesus, that day will be like coming to "trees and hills they long have known." But those who don't know him will be carried away, like chaff in the wind. The unrighteous will not be able to withstand that judgment. Since one of two destinies await all people on that day, we would be wise to give our life to Jesus during these days.

## INTERACTION ⟨AND⟩ REFLECTION

- We will one day give an account before God. How important is it to be called "blessed," or "approved by God"?
- In our reading today, what words and images does the psalmist use to describe the righteous person?

## 3 THE REDEMPTION OF OUR BODIES (32.2)
### Job 19:23–27

The famous preacher John Stott got tired of people complimenting him by saying, "Oh, you must have love and passion for *souls!*" In his heart, John Stott knew they only had it half right. He said, "I have never had a love or passion for souls. . . . What God has done is create human beings, and human beings are more than a soul: they are body-souls and they are body-souls-in-a-community."[2] This was a wise thing to say. Job would agree with him too. Job was glad to know that, even though death would destroy his skin, in his flesh he would see God again! When Jesus returns, everyone who died believing in him will have his or her body reunited with his or her soul, and both body and soul will dwell with God forever. Isn't that great news? It should help us whenever we attend a Christian's

---

2. John R. W. Stott, *Walk in His Shoes: The Compassion of Jesus* (London: IVP, 1975), 16.

funeral. The separation of the body from the soul is only temporary. When Jesus saves us, he does more than save our *souls*—he saves our *bodies* from the penalty of sin too!

## INTERACTION AND REFLECTION

- How is your love for God strengthened by knowing that he saves your body and your soul?
- Name some things that you can do to take better care of your body and soul.

# |||||||||||||||||||||| *Lesson* 33 ||||||||||||||||||||||

# THE LAST JUDGMENT

## 1 THE SUPREME JUDGE (33.1)
*Psalm 2*

Do you enjoy watching movies? What two movies would you list as all-time favorites? Because movies are so fun to watch, sometimes we never want the movie to end. We wish it would go on forever. But it doesn't. Eventually the end credits come onto the screen. Sadly, we can sometimes view life the way we view movies. We begin to think that life as we know it will go on forever, that it will keep on going from one generation to another without end. Psalm 2 teaches us something different. One day God's anointed King, the Lord Jesus, will come again to take the ends of the earth as his rightful possession. This psalm warns us to be wise—to honor the Son, serve the Lord with fear, and take refuge in him before his wrath comes. Have you submitted your life to God's King yet? Remember, the Scriptures are clear: eventually the end credits will roll across the screen of human history.

## INTERACTION ⟨AND⟩ REFLECTION

- In this lesson you will come to the end of *Big Beliefs!* What important truth did you learn today that should stay with you forever?
- We don't know the exact day that Jesus will return. Until then, how should we be living our lives?

## 2 THE FINAL VERDICTS (33.2)
### Revelation 20:11–15

Joey got up out of the mud and spoke on behalf of his friends who were with him. His words came slowly and with a sarcastic drawl: "Awww, Mr. Robinson. Can't we have just one more chance? Pretty please?" "No," said Mr. Robinson. "If I've told you once, I've told you a thousand times, stay out of the sandlot after a big rain. It ruins the playing field. So it's over now—this is my final word—you can't play here anymore!" Then Mr. Robinson turned and spoke to the other children who had stayed off the sandlot. "For all of you who listened to my warning, you get to come with me. There's a better field you can play on. I'll take you there."

This story is an illustration of our Bible reading today. When Jesus returns, there will be no more chances to repent of sin and believe in Jesus as the Savior. The verdict will be final. Some people will be taken away, while those who followed Jesus Christ will enter the new heaven and earth. This is true. The Bible tells us this over and over. So, I ask you, what will you do with Jesus?

## INTERACTION AND REFLECTION

- There are only two answers to the question, "What will you do with Jesus?" What are the two different answers? What is your answer?
- Does knowing about the final judgment make you want to turn to Christ for forgiveness of sins?

## 3 COME, LORD JESUS (33.3)
### Revelation 22:12–21

How do you feel at bedtime on Christmas Eve, when you know that Christmas Day will come the next morning? Most of us are excited and eager because we have been looking forward to Christmas for many months—maybe the whole year! Wouldn't it be great if we felt the same way about the day when Jesus returns? We get really excited about celebrating the day Jesus was born, because Christmas is a fun time of opening presents, drinking hot chocolate, and being with our family. But we should be even more excited about the day when Jesus will come again. On that day Jesus will take us to heaven and we will partake in a great banquet feast. Then, God will create a new earth with no sadness and no hurt. The apostle John, who wrote the last book in the Bible, looked forward to Jesus's return. To show how much he longed for that long-awaited day, he exclaimed, "Come, Lord Jesus!" (v. 21). If we knew how great his return will be for his children, we would be shouting cheers like the apostle John: "Come! Bring it on! Hurry up, Lord Jesus!" All history is moving toward that wonderful day, and we have been waiting a very long time for it. May the grace of our Lord Jesus be with you all. Now, on that day, and forever more. Amen.

## INTERACTION AND REFLECTION

- Why should you be looking forward to the return of Jesus? Take time to celebrate!
- You have finished *Big Beliefs!* We hope this has been helpful to you and your family.

# The Westminster Confession of Faith

## Chapter 1

# THE HOLY SCRIPTURE

1.1. Although the light of nature and the works of creation and providence manifest the goodness, wisdom, and power of God, to such an extent that men are without excuse, yet they are not sufficient to give that knowledge of God and of his will which is necessary for salvation. Therefore it pleased the Lord, at various times and in diverse ways, to reveal himself and to declare his will to his church; and afterward—for the better preserving and propagating of the truth, and for the more sure establishment and comfort of the church against the corruption of the flesh and the malice of Satan and of the world—to commit this revelation wholly to writing. Therefore the Holy Scripture is most necessary, God's former ways of revealing his will to his people having ceased.

1.2. Under the name of Holy Scripture, or the written Word of God, are all the books of the Old and New Testaments, namely:

### THE OLD TESTAMENT

Genesis

Exodus

Leviticus

Numbers

Deuteronomy

Joshua

Judges

Ruth

1 Samuel

2 Samuel

1 Kings

2 Kings

1 Chronicles

2 Chronicles

Ezra

Nehemiah

Esther

Job

Psalms

Proverbs

Ecclesiastes
The Song of Songs
Isaiah
Jeremiah
Lamentations
Ezekiel
Daniel
Hosea
Joel
Amos

Obadiah
Jonah
Micah
Nahum
Habakkuk
Zephaniah
Haggai
Zechariah
Malachi

## THE NEW TESTAMENT

The Gospels according to
  Matthew
  Mark
  Luke
  John
The Acts of the Apostles
The Epistles of Paul:
  Romans
  1 Corinthians
  2 Corinthians
  Galatians
  Ephesians
  Philippians
  Colossians
  1 Thessalonians

2 Thessalonians
1 Timothy
2 Timothy
Titus
Philemon
The Epistle to
  the Hebrews
The Epistle of James
The first and second
  Epistles of Peter
The first, second, and
  third Epistles of John
The Epistle of Jude
The Revelation

All these are given by inspiration of God to be the rule of faith and life.

1.3. The books commonly called the Apocrypha, because they are not divinely inspired, are not part of the canon of Scripture, and therefore are of no authority in the church of God and are not to be approved, or made use of, in any manner different from other human writings.

1.4. The authority of the Holy Scripture, because of which it ought to be believed and obeyed, does not depend upon the testimony of any man or church, but entirely upon God, its author (who is truth itself); therefore it is to be received, because it is the Word of God.

1.5. We may be moved and induced by the testimony of the church to a high and reverent esteem for the Holy Scripture. The heavenly character of its content, the efficacy of its doctrine, the majesty of its style, the agreement of all its parts, the scope of the whole (which is to give all glory to God), the full disclosure it makes of the only way of man's salvation, its many other incomparable excellencies, and its entire perfection, are arguments by which it gives abundant evidence that it is the Word of God. Nevertheless, our full persuasion and assurance of its infallible truth and divine authority is from the inward work of the Holy Spirit bearing witness by and with the Word in our hearts.

1.6. The whole counsel of God concerning all things necessary for his own glory and man's salvation, faith, and life, is either expressly stated in Scripture or by good and necessary inference may be deduced from Scripture, unto which nothing at any time is to be added, whether by new revelations of the Spirit or by traditions of men. Nevertheless, we acknowledge that the inward illumination of the Spirit of God is necessary for the saving understanding of such things as are revealed in the Word. We also acknowledge that there are some circumstances concerning the worship of God and the government of the church—circumstances common to human activities and societies—which are to be ordered by the light of nature and Christian prudence, according to the general rules of the Word, which are always to be observed.

1.7. Not all things in Scripture are equally plain in themselves or equally clear to all; yet those things which are necessary to be known, believed, and observed for salvation are so clearly stated and explained in one place or another in Scripture, that not only the educated but also the uneducated may gain a sufficient understanding of them by a proper use of the ordinary means.

1.8. The Old Testament in Hebrew (which was the native language of the people of God of old) and the New Testament in Greek (which at the time it was written was the language most generally known to the nations), being directly inspired by God and by his unique care and providence kept pure in all ages, are therefore authoritative, so that in all controversies of religion the church is finally to appeal to them. But, because these original languages are not understood by all the people of God, who have a right to, and a vital interest in, the Scriptures and are commanded to read and search them in the fear of God, therefore the Scriptures are to be translated into the common language of every nation to which they come; so that, the Word of God dwelling abundantly in all, they may worship him in an acceptable manner and by perseverance and the encouragement of the Scriptures may have hope.

1.9. The infallible rule of interpretation of Scripture is the Scripture itself. Therefore, when there is a question about the true and full meaning of any Scripture (which is not manifold, but one), that meaning must be searched out and ascertained by other places that speak more clearly.

1.10. The supreme judge by whom all controversies of religion are to be settled and all decrees of councils, opinions of ancient writers, doctrines of men, and claims to private revelations are to be examined, can be only the Holy Spirit speaking in the Scripture. With his decision we are to be satisfied.

## Chapter 2

# GOD AND THE
# HOLY TRINITY

2.1. There is only one living and true God, who is infinite in being and perfection. He is a most pure spirit, invisible, with neither body, parts, nor passive properties. He is unchangeable, boundless, eternal, and incomprehensible. He is almighty, most wise, most holy, most free, and most absolute. He works all things according to the counsel of his own unchangeable and most righteous will, for his own glory. He is most loving, gracious, merciful, long-suffering, abundant in goodness and truth, forgiving iniquity, transgression, and sin, and he is the rewarder of those who diligently seek him. He is also most just and terrifying in his judgments, hating all sin, and will by no means acquit the guilty.

2.2. God has all life, glory, goodness, and blessedness in and of himself. He alone is all-sufficient, in and to himself, not standing in need of any creatures which he has made, nor deriving any glory from them, but rather manifesting his own glory in, by, to, and on them. He alone is the fountain of all being, of whom, through whom, and to whom are all things. He has absolute sovereignty over them, to do by them, for them, or upon them whatever he pleases. In his sight all things are open and manifest; his knowledge is infinite, infallible, and independent of his creatures; so that nothing to him is contingent or uncertain. He is most holy in all his counsels, in all his works, and in all his commands. To him is due from angels and men, and every other creature, whatever worship, service, or obedience he is pleased to require of them.

2.3. In the unity of the Godhead there are three persons, of one substance, power, and eternity: God the Father, God the Son, and God the Holy Spirit. The Father is of none, neither begotten nor proceeding; the Son is eternally begotten of the Father; the Holy Spirit eternally proceeds from the Father and the Son.

# Chapter 3

# GOD'S ETERNAL DECREE

3.1. God, from all eternity, did—by the most wise and holy counsel of his own will—freely and unchangeably ordain whatever comes to pass. Yet he ordered all things in such a way that he is not the author of sin, nor does he force his creatures to act against their wills; neither is the liberty or contingency of second causes taken away, but rather established.

3.2. Although God knows whatever may or can come to pass under all conceivable conditions, yet he has not decreed anything because he foresaw it as future or as that which would come to pass under such conditions.

3.3. By God's decree, for the manifestation of his glory, some men and angels are predestined to everlasting life, and others are foreordained to everlasting death.

3.4. These angels and men, thus predestined and foreordained, are individually and unchangeably designated, and their number is so certain and definite that it cannot be either increased or decreased.

3.5. Those people who are predestined to life, God—before the foundation of the world was laid, according to his eternal and unchangeable purpose and the secret counsel and good pleasure of his will—has chosen in Christ to everlasting glory. He chose them out of his free grace and love alone, not because he foresaw faith, or good works, or perseverance in either of these, or anything else in the creature, as conditions or causes moving him to do this; and all to the praise of his glorious grace.

3.6. As God has appointed the elect to glory, so he has—by the eternal and most free purpose of his will—foreordained all the means to that end. Therefore, his chosen ones, all of them being fallen in Adam, are redeemed by Christ and are effectually called to faith in Christ by his Spirit working in due season. They are justified, adopted, sanctified, and kept by his power, through faith, unto salvation. No others are redeemed by Christ, effectually called, justified, adopted, sanctified, and saved, except the elect only.

3.7. The rest of mankind God was pleased—according to the unsearchable counsel of his own will, whereby he extends or withholds mercy as he pleases—for the glory of his sovereign power over his creatures, to pass by; and to ordain them to dishonor and wrath for their sin, to the praise of his glorious justice.

3.8. The doctrine of this high mystery of predestination is to be handled with special prudence and care, so that men, taking heed to the will of God revealed in his Word and yielding obedience to it, may—from the certainty of their effectual calling—be assured of their eternal election. Thus, this doctrine shall provide reason for praise, reverence, and admiration of God; and for humility, diligence, and abundant consolation to all who sincerely obey the gospel.

## Chapter 4

# CREATION

4.1. It pleased God the Father, Son, and Holy Spirit, for the manifestation of the glory of his eternal power, wisdom, and goodness, in the beginning, to create—or make out of nothing—the world and everything in it, whether visible or invisible, in the space of six days, and all very good.

4.2. After God had made everything else, he created mankind. He made them male and female, with rational and immortal souls, endowed with knowledge, righteousness, and true holiness, after his own image. They had the law of God written in their hearts and had power to fulfill it. They were, however, under a possibility of transgressing, being left to the liberty of their own will, which was subject to change. In addition to this law written in their hearts, they received a command not to eat of the tree of the knowledge of good and evil. As long as they obeyed this command, they were happy in their communion with God and had dominion over the creatures.

# Chapter 5

# PROVIDENCE

5.1. God—the great Creator of all things—upholds, directs, disposes, and governs all creatures, actions, and things, from the greatest even to the least. He exercises this most wise and holy providence according to his infallible foreknowledge and the free and unchangeable counsel of his own will, to the praise of the glory of his wisdom, power, justice, goodness, and mercy.

5.2. Although—in relation to the foreknowledge and decree of God, the first Cause—all things come to pass unchangeably and infallibly; yet, by the same providence, he orders them to occur according to the nature of second causes, either necessarily, freely, or contingently.

5.3. In his ordinary providence, God makes use of means, yet he is free to work without, above, and against them as he pleases.

5.4. The almighty power, unsearchable wisdom, and infinite goodness of God manifest themselves so completely in his providence that it extends even to the first fall and all other sins of angels and men—not by a bare permission, but by a permission which has joined with it a most wise and powerful limiting, and otherwise ordering and governing of them in a varied administration, for his own holy purposes. However, the sinfulness comes from the creatures alone and not from God, who, because he is most holy and righteous, neither is nor can be the author or approver of sin.

5.5. The most wise, righteous, and gracious God often leaves his own children, for a time, to manifold temptations and to the corruption of their own hearts. He does this to chastise them for their past sins, to humble them by making them aware of the hidden strength of the corruption and deceitfulness of their hearts, and then to raise them to a closer, more constant dependence upon himself for their support, to make them more watchful against all future occasions for sinning, and to fulfill various other just and holy purposes.

5.6. As for those wicked and ungodly men whom God, as a righteous judge, blinds and hardens because of their past sins, God withholds his grace, by which their minds might have been enlightened and their hearts affected. He also sometimes takes away the gifts which they had, and exposes them to such things as their corrupt nature makes into occasions for sinning. Moreover, he gives them over to their own lusts, the temptations of the world, and the power of Satan, by which they harden themselves even under the same means which God uses to soften others.

5.7. As, in general, the providence of God reaches to all creatures, so, in a very special way, it cares for his church and disposes all things for its good.

## Chapter 6

# THE FALL OF MAN, AND SIN
# AND ITS PUNISHMENT

6.1. Our first parents, being seduced by the subtlety and temptation of Satan, sinned in eating the forbidden fruit. God was pleased to permit this sin of theirs, according to his wise and holy counsel, because his purpose was, through it, to glorify himself.

6.2. By this sin they fell from their original righteousness and communion with God, and so became dead in sin and wholly defiled in all the parts and faculties of soul and body.

6.3. Since they were the root of all mankind, the guilt of this sin was imputed to—and the same death in sin and corrupted nature were conveyed to—all their posterity descending from them by ordinary generation.

6.4. From this original corruption, by which we are utterly disinclined, disabled, and antagonistic to all that is good and wholly inclined to all that is evil, all actual transgressions proceed.

6.5. During this life, this corruption of nature remains in those who are regenerated. Even though it is pardoned and put to death through Christ, yet both this corruption of nature and all its expressions are in fact really sin.

6.6. Every sin—both original and actual—is a transgression of the righteous law of God and contrary to it. Therefore, every sin in its own nature brings guilt upon the sinner, on account of which he is bound over to the holy wrath of God and the curse of the law. Consequently, he is subject to death, with all miseries—spiritual, temporal, and eternal.

## Chapter 7

# GOD'S COVENANT WITH MAN

7.1. The distance between God and the creature is so great that, even though rational creatures are responsible to obey him as their Creator, yet they could never experience any enjoyment of him as their blessing and reward except by way of some voluntary condescension on his part, which he has been pleased to express by way of covenant.

7.2. The first covenant made with man was a covenant of works in which life was promised to Adam and, in him, to his posterity, upon condition of perfect and personal obedience.

7.3. Since man, by his fall, made himself incapable of life by that covenant, the Lord was then pleased to make a second covenant, commonly called the covenant of grace. In it God freely offers life and salvation by Jesus Christ to sinners, requiring of them faith in him, that they may be saved, and promising to give his Holy Spirit to all those who are ordained to eternal life, to make them willing and able to believe.

7.4. This covenant of grace is sometimes presented in the Scriptures by the name of a will or testament, with reference to the death of Jesus Christ (the testator) and to the everlasting inheritance—with all that belongs to it—bequeathed in it.

7.5. In the time of the law, this covenant was administered differently than in the time of the gospel. Under the law, it was administered by promises, prophecies, sacrifices, circumcision, the passover lamb, and other types and ordinances given to the Jewish people, all of which foreshadowed Christ to come. These were, for that time, sufficient and efficacious, through the work of the Spirit, to instruct and build up the elect in their faith in the promised Messiah, by whom they received complete forgiveness of sins and eternal salvation. This covenant administration is called the old testament.

7.6. Under the gospel, Christ (the reality) having been revealed, the ordinances by which this covenant is dispensed are the preaching of the Word and the administration of the sacraments of baptism and the Lord's supper. Although these are fewer in number and are administered with more simplicity and less outward glory, yet in them the covenant is set forth in greater fullness, clarity, and spiritual efficacy to all nations, both Jews and Gentiles, and is called the new testament. Therefore, there are not two covenants of grace differing in substance, but only one, under various administrations.

# Chapter 8

# CHRIST THE MEDIATOR

8.1. God was pleased, in his eternal purpose, to choose and ordain the Lord Jesus, his only begotten Son, to be the mediator between God and man. As the mediator, he is the prophet, priest, and king, the Head and Savior of the church, the heir of all things, and the judge of the world. God gave to him, from all eternity, a people to be his seed and to be by him, in time, redeemed, called, justified, sanctified, and glorified.

8.2. The Son of God, the second person of the Trinity, being truly and eternally God, of one substance and equal with the Father, did, when the fullness of time had come, take upon himself man's nature, with all its essential properties and common frailties, yet without sin. He was conceived by the power of the Holy Spirit in the womb of the virgin Mary and of her substance. In this way, two whole natures, the divine and the human, perfect and distinct, were inseparably joined together in one person without being changed, mixed, or confused. This person is truly God and truly man, yet one Christ, the only mediator between God and man.

8.3. In his human nature, united to the divine nature, the Lord Jesus was set apart and anointed with the Holy Spirit beyond measure, having in him all the treasures of wisdom and knowledge. In him the Father was pleased to have all fullness dwell, so that—being holy, blameless, and undefiled, full of grace and truth—he might be completely equipped to fulfill the office of a mediator and guarantor. He did not take this office to himself but was called to it by his Father, who put all power and judgment into his hand and commanded him to execute it.

8.4. This office the Lord Jesus most willingly undertook, and in order to discharge its obligations he was born under the law and perfectly fulfilled it. He endured most grievous torments in his soul and most painful sufferings in his body; he was crucified, died, and was buried; he remained under the power of death, yet his body did not undergo decay; and he arose from the dead on the third day with the same body in which he had suffered. In this body he ascended into heaven, where he sits at the right hand of his Father, making intercession, and he shall return to judge men and angels at the end of the age.

8.5. The Lord Jesus, by his perfect obedience and sacrifice of himself—which he through the eternal Spirit once offered up to God—has fully satisfied the justice of his Father. He purchased not only reconciliation but also an everlasting inheritance in the kingdom of heaven for all those whom the Father has given to him.

8.6. Although the work of redemption was not actually accomplished by Christ until after his incarnation, yet the power, efficacy, and benefits of it were applied to the elect in all ages successively from the beginning of the world, in and by those promises, types, and sacrifices by which Christ was revealed and signified to be the seed of the woman who would bruise the serpent's head, and to be the Lamb slain from the beginning of the world. He is the same yesterday, today, and forever.

8.7. In the work of mediation, Christ acts according to both natures. Each nature does what is proper to itself; yet, by reason of the unity of his person, that which is proper to one nature is in Scripture sometimes attributed to the person designated by the other nature.

8.8. To all those for whom Christ purchased redemption, he certainly and effectually applies and communicates it. He makes intercession for them and reveals to them, in and by the Word, the mysteries of salvation. He effectually persuades them by his Spirit to believe and obey, and governs their hearts by his Word and Spirit. He overcomes all their enemies by his almighty power and wisdom in such a manner, and by such ways, as are most agreeable to his wonderful and unsearchable administration.

## Chapter 9

# FREE WILL

9.1. God has endowed the will of man with such natural liberty that it is neither forced nor—by any absolute necessity of nature—determined to good or evil.

9.2. Man, in his state of innocence, had freedom and ability to will and to do what was good and well-pleasing to God, and yet not unalterably, so that he might fall from it.

9.3. Man, by his fall into a state of sin, has completely lost all ability to choose any spiritual good that accompanies salvation. Therefore, an unregenerate man, because he is opposed to that good and is dead in sin, is unable by his own strength to convert himself or to prepare himself to be converted.

9.4. When God converts a sinner and brings him into the state of grace, he frees him from his natural bondage to sin, and by his grace alone he enables him freely to will and to do what is spiritually good. Yet, because of his remaining corruption, he does not perfectly nor only will what is good, but also wills what is evil.

9.5. The will of man is made perfectly and unchangeably free to do good alone, only in the state of glory.

## Chapter 10

# EFFECTUAL CALLING

10.1. All those—and only those—whom God has predestined to life, he is pleased to call effectually in his appointed and accepted time, by his Word and Spirit. He calls them from the state of sin and death—in which they are by nature—to grace and salvation by Jesus Christ. In this calling, God enlightens their minds spiritually and savingly, so that they understand the things of God. He takes away their hearts of stone and gives them hearts of flesh, renews their wills, and by his almighty power turns them to what is good and effectually draws them to Jesus Christ. Yet he does this in such a way that they come most freely, being made willing by his grace.

10.2. This effectual call is from God's free and special grace alone, and not from anything at all that God foresees in man, who is entirely passive in it, until—being made alive and renewed by the Holy Spirit—he is enabled to answer the call and embrace the grace offered and conveyed in it.

10.3. Elect infants who die in infancy are regenerated and saved by Christ through the Spirit, who works when, where, and how he pleases. So also are all other elect persons who are incapable of being outwardly called by the ministry of the Word.

10.4. Although other persons who are not elected may be called by the ministry of the Word and may experience some common operations of the Spirit, yet they never really come to Christ and therefore cannot be saved. Much less can men not professing to be Christians be saved in any other way, no matter how carefully they may order their lives by the light of nature and by the laws of whatever religion they profess. To assert and maintain that they may be saved in some other way is very pernicious and is to be detested.

## Chapter 11

# JUSTIFICATION

11.1. Those whom God effectually calls he also freely justifies, not by infusing righteousness into them, but by pardoning their sins and by accounting and accepting them as righteous. It is not for anything wrought in them, or done by them, but for Christ's sake alone that they are justified. It is not by imputing faith itself, the act of believing, or any other act of Christian obedience to them, as their righteousness, but by imputing the obedience and satisfaction of Christ to them who receive and rest on him and his righteousness by faith. Men do not have this faith of themselves; it is the gift of God.

11.2. Faith—receiving and resting on Christ and his righteousness—is the only instrument of justification; yet it is not the only grace in the person justified, but is always accompanied by all other saving graces. Justifying faith is not dead, but works by love.

11.3. Christ, by his obedience and death, fully discharged the debt of all those who are justified. He made a proper, real, and full satisfaction to his Father's justice in their behalf. Yet, because he was freely given by the Father for them, and because his obedience and satisfaction were freely accepted in their stead, and not for anything in them, their justification is only of free grace. It was God's purpose in the justification of sinners to glorify both his exact justice and his rich grace.

11.4. God, from all eternity, decreed to justify all the elect. In the fullness of time, Christ died for their sins and rose again for their justification. Nevertheless, they are not justified until, in due time, the Holy Spirit actually applies Christ to them.

11.5. God continues to forgive the sins of those who are justified. Although they can never fall from the state of justification, yet they may by their sins fall under God's fatherly displeasure and not have the light of his countenance restored to them until they humble themselves, confess their sin, plead for pardon, and renew their faith and repentance.

11.6. The justification of believers under the old testament was, in all these respects, one and the same with the justification of believers under the new testament.

## Chapter 12

# ADOPTION

12.1. All those who are justified God graciously guarantees to make partakers of the grace of adoption in and for his only Son, Jesus Christ. By this act they are taken into the number of God's children and enjoy the liberties and privileges of that relationship; they are given his name; they receive the Spirit of adoption; they have access to the throne of grace with boldness; and they are enabled to cry, "Abba, Father." Like a father, God has compassion on, protects, provides for, and chastens them; yet, they will never be cast off, but are sealed to the day of redemption, and will inherit the promises as heirs of everlasting salvation.

## Chapter 13

# SANCTIFICATION

13.1. Those who are effectually called and regenerated, having a new heart and a new spirit created in them, are further sanctified—truly and personally—through the power of Christ's death and resurrection, by his Word and Spirit dwelling in them. The dominion of the whole body of sin is destroyed, its various lusts are more and more weakened and put to death, and those called and regenerated are more and more enlivened and strengthened in all saving graces, leading to the practice of true holiness, without which no man shall see the Lord.

13.2. This sanctification, although imperfect in this life, is effected in every part of man's nature. Some remnants of corruption still persist in every part, and so there arises a continual and irreconcilable war—the flesh warring against the Spirit, and the Spirit against the flesh.

13.3. Although in this war the remaining corruption may strongly prevail for a time, yet, through the continual supply of strength from the sanctifying Spirit of Christ, the regenerate nature overcomes, and so the saints grow in grace, perfecting holiness in the fear of God.

## Chapter 14

# SAVING FAITH

14.1. The grace of faith, by which the elect are enabled to believe to the saving of their souls, is the work of the Spirit of Christ in their hearts, and is ordinarily produced through the ministry of the Word. This faith is increased and strengthened by the same means, and also by the administration of the sacraments and prayer.

14.2. By this faith, a Christian believes to be true whatever is revealed in the Word, because of the authority of God himself speaking in it. He also responds differently to what each particular passage contains—obeying the commands, trembling at the threatenings, and embracing the promises of God for this life and that which is to come. But the principal acts of saving faith are accepting, receiving, and resting upon Christ alone for justification, sanctification, and eternal life, by virtue of the covenant of grace.

14.3. This faith varies in degrees. It may be weak or strong. It may often, and in many ways, be assailed and weakened, but it gains the victory. It matures in many to the attainment of a full assurance through Christ, who is both the author and the perfecter of our faith.

## Chapter 15

# REPENTANCE UNTO LIFE

15.1. Repentance unto life is a gospel grace, the doctrine of which is to be preached by every minister of the gospel, just as is the doctrine of faith in Christ.

15.2. By it a sinner—seeing and sensing not only the danger but also the filthiness and hatefulness of his sins, because they are contrary to God's holy nature and his righteous law—turns from all his sins to God in the realization that God promises mercy in Christ to those who repent, and so grieves for and hates his sins that he determines and endeavors to walk with God in all the ways that he commands.

15.3. Although repentance is not to be relied on as any payment of the penalty for sin, or any cause of the pardon of sin (which is God's act of free grace in Christ); yet repentance is so necessary for all sinners, that no one may expect pardon without it.

15.4. No sin is so small that it does not deserve damnation. Nor is any sin so great that it can bring damnation upon those who truly repent.

15.5. No one should be satisfied with a general repentance; rather, it is everyone's duty to endeavor to repent of each particular sin, particularly.

15.6. It is the duty of each one to make private confession of his sins to God, praying for pardon (and whoever confesses his sins, prays for forgiveness, and forsakes those sins shall find mercy). Similarly, anyone who has scandalized a brother, or the church of Christ, ought to be willing by private or public confession, and sorrow for his sin, to declare his repentance to those that are offended, who are then to be reconciled to him and receive him in love.

## Chapter 16

# GOOD WORKS

16.1. Good works are only such as God has commanded in his holy Word, and not such as, without the warrant of Scripture, are devised by men out of blind zeal or any pretense of good intention.

16.2. These good works, done in obedience to God's commandments, are the fruits and evidences of a true and living faith. By them believers show their thankfulness, strengthen their assurance, build up their fellow believers, adorn the profession of the gospel, shut the mouths of the adversaries, and glorify God. They are his workmanship, created in Christ Jesus for good works, so that, bearing fruit unto holiness, they may attain the outcome, which is eternal life.

16.3. Their ability to do good works is not at all from themselves, but entirely from the Spirit of Christ. And—in order that they may be enabled to do these things—besides the graces believers have already received, there must also be an actual influence of the same Holy Spirit working in them both to will and to do God's good pleasure. This truth, however, should not cause believers to become negligent, as though they were not bound to perform any duty without a special moving of the Spirit; rather, they ought to be diligent in stirring up the grace of God that is in them.

16.4. Those who attain the greatest heights of obedience possible in this life are so far from being able to go beyond duty and to do more than God requires, that they fall short of much that is their duty to do.

16.5. We cannot, by our best works, merit forgiveness for sin or eternal life at the hand of God. This is true because of the great disproportion between our best works and the glory to come, and because of the infinite distance between us and God. We cannot benefit God by our best works nor render satisfaction for the debt of our former sins, for when we have done all we can, we have done merely our duty and are unprofitable servants. This is because, insofar as they are good, these deeds proceed from the Spirit; and, insofar as they are done by us, they are defiled and mixed with so much weakness and imperfection that they cannot endure the severity of God's judgment.

16.6. Nevertheless, because believers are accepted through Christ, their good works are also accepted in him. They are accepted not because believers are in this life unblamable and unreprovable in God's sight, but because he, looking upon them in his Son, is pleased to accept and reward that which is sincere, even though it is accompanied by many weaknesses and imperfections.

16.7. Although the works done by unregenerate men may in themselves be things which God commands and things which are useful to themselves and others, yet—because they do not come from a heart purified by faith, are not done in a right manner according to the Word, and are not done for the right purpose, which is to glorify God—they are therefore sinful, and cannot please God or make one suitable to receive his grace. Yet, neglecting them is even more sinful and displeasing to God.

## Chapter 17

# THE PERSEVERANCE
# OF THE SAINTS

17.1. Those whom God has accepted in his Beloved, effectually called, and sanctified by his Spirit, can neither totally nor finally fall away from the state of grace, but shall certainly persevere in it to the end and be eternally saved.

17.2. The perseverance of the saints does not depend upon their own free will, but on the unchangeableness of the decree of election, flowing from the free and unchangeable love of God the Father; on the efficacy of the merit and intercession of Jesus Christ; on the continuing presence of the Spirit and the seed of God within them; and on the nature of the covenant of grace. These are grounds of the certainty and infallibility of their perseverance.

17.3. Nevertheless, they may—through the temptations of Satan and of the world, the pervasiveness of the corruption remaining in them, and the neglect of the means by which they are to be preserved—fall into grievous sins and for a time continue in them. In so doing they incur God's displeasure and grieve his Holy Spirit; some measure of God's graces and comforts is taken from them; they have their hearts hardened and their consciences wounded; they harm others and give them occasion to sin, and bring temporal judgments upon themselves.

## Chapter 18

# THE ASSURANCE OF GRACE
# AND SALVATION

18.1. Although hypocrites and other unregenerate men may vainly deceive themselves with false hopes and fleshly presumptions that they are in God's favor and in a state of salvation, this hope of theirs will perish. Nevertheless, those who truly believe on the Lord Jesus, love him sincerely, and strive to live in all good conscience before him, may in this life be certainly assured that they are in the state of grace and may rejoice in the hope of the glory of God, a hope that shall never make them ashamed.

18.2. This certainty is not merely a conjectural and probable persuasion grounded on a fallible hope, but an infallible assurance of faith, founded on the divine truth of the promises of salvation, on the evidence in our hearts that the promised graces are present, and on the fact that the Spirit of adoption witnesses with our spirits that we are God's children. The Holy Spirit, by whom we are sealed for the day of redemption, is the pledge of our inheritance.

18.3. This infallible assurance does not so belong to the essence of faith but that a true believer may wait long and contend with many difficulties before he partakes of it. Yet, because he is enabled by the Spirit to know the things which are freely given to him by God, he may—without any extraordinary revelation—attain this assurance by a proper use of the ordinary means. It is therefore the duty of everyone to be very diligent in making certain that God has called and chosen him. By such diligence his heart may grow in peace and joy in the Holy Spirit, in love and thankfulness to God, and in strength and cheerfulness in the duties which obedience to God requires—the proper fruits of this assurance. Thus it is far from inclining men to carelessness.

18.4. True believers may have the assurance of their salvation shaken, diminished, or temporarily lost in various ways: as by negligence in preserving it, by falling into some special sin which wounds the conscience and grieves the Spirit, by some sudden or violent temptation, or by God's withdrawing the light of his countenance and allowing even those who reverence him to walk in darkness and have no light. Yet, true believers are never completely deprived of that seed of God and life of faith, that love for Christ and fellow believers, that sincerity of heart and conscience concerning duty, out of which—by the operation of the Spirit—this assurance may in due time be revived; and by which, in the meantime, they are supported from utter despair.

## Chapter 19

# THE LAW OF GOD

19.1. God gave Adam a law, in the form of a covenant of works, by which he bound him and all his descendants to personal, entire, exact, and perpetual obedience. He promised life if Adam kept the law and threatened death if he broke it. Moreover, he endowed Adam with power and ability to keep that law.

19.2. This law, after Adam fell, continued to be a perfect rule of righteousness and, as such, was given by God upon Mount Sinai in ten commandments written on two stone tablets. The first four commandments contain our duty to God, the other six our duty to man.

19.3. In addition to this law, commonly called the moral law, God was pleased to give the people of Israel—as the church under age—ceremonial laws, which contained several typological ordinances. These ordinances consisted partly of worship, prefiguring Christ, his graces, actions, sufferings, and benefits, and partly of various instructions of moral duties. All these ceremonial laws are now abrogated under the new testament.

19.4. To the people of Israel, as a civil entity, he also gave various judicial laws which expired at the time their State expired. Therefore, these judicial laws place no obligation upon anyone now, except as they embody general principles of justice.

19.5. The moral law binds all people at all times to obedience, both those who are justified and those who are not. The obligation to obey the moral law is not only because of its content, but also because of the authority of God the Creator, who gave it. In the gospel, Christ in no way dissolves this obligation, but greatly strengthens it.

19.6. Although true believers are not under the law as a covenant of works by which they are justified or condemned, nevertheless the law is of great use to them as well as to others. By informing them—as a rule of life—both of the will of God and of their duty, it directs and binds them to walk accordingly. It also reveals to them the sinful pollutions of their nature, hearts, and lives. Therefore, when they examine themselves in the light of the law, they may come to further conviction of, humiliation for, and hatred of their sin, together with a clearer view of their need of Christ and the perfection of his obedience. The law is also useful to the regenerate because, by forbidding sin, it restrains their corruptions. By its threats it shows them what their sins deserve, and, although they are free from the curse threatened in the law, it shows the afflictions that they may expect because of them in this life. The promises of the law likewise show to the regenerate God's approval of obedience and the blessings they may expect as they obey the law, although these blessings are not due to them by the law as a covenant of works. Therefore, the fact that a man does good rather than evil because the law encourages good and discourages evil is no evidence that the man is under the law rather than under grace.

19.7. These uses of the law do not conflict with the grace of the gospel, but are in complete harmony with it; for it is the Spirit of Christ who subdues and enables the will of man to do freely and cheerfully those things which the will of God, revealed in the law, requires.

*Chapter 20*

# CHRISTIAN LIBERTY AND LIBERTY OF CONSCIENCE

20.1. The liberty which Christ purchased for believers under the gospel consists in their freedom from the guilt of sin, from the condemning wrath of God, and from the curse of the moral law. Furthermore, it consists in their being delivered from this present evil age, from bondage to Satan and the dominion of sin, from the evil of afflictions, from the sting of death, from the victory of the grave, and from everlasting damnation. It consists also in their free access to God and in yielding obedience to him, not out of slavish fear, but out of a childlike love and willing mind. All of these things were common to believers also under the law. Under the new testament, however, the liberty of Christians is further enlarged: they are free from the yoke of the ceremonial law to which the Jewish church was subjected; they have greater boldness of access to the throne of grace; and they experience in greater measure the gifts of God's free Spirit than believers under the law ordinarily partook of.

20.2. God alone is Lord of the conscience and has left it free from the doctrines and commandments of men which are—in anything— contrary to his Word, or which—in matters of faith or worship—are in addition to it. Therefore, anyone who believes such doctrines or obeys such commands out of conscience betrays true liberty of conscience. The requiring of an implicit faith, and an absolute and blind obedience, destroys both liberty of conscience and reason.

20.3. Those who, on the pretext of Christian liberty, practice any sin or cherish any evil desire destroy the purpose of Christian liberty. This purpose is that, having been delivered out of the hand of our enemies, we may serve the Lord without fear, in holiness and righteousness before him all the days of our life.

20.4. Because the powers which God has ordained and the liberty which Christ has purchased are not intended by God to destroy each other, but mutually to uphold and preserve one another, those who, in the name of Christian liberty, oppose any lawful power or any lawful exercise of it, whether civil or ecclesiastical, resist the ordinance of God. Those who declare opinions or maintain practices contrary to the light of nature, or to the known principles of Christianity (whether concerning faith, worship, or manner of life), or the power of godliness; or who are guilty of such erroneous opinions or practices, as either in their own nature, or in the manner of publishing or maintaining them, are destructive of the external peace and order which Christ has established in the church, may lawfully be called to account, and proceeded against, by the censures of the church.

## Chapter 21

# RELIGIOUS WORSHIP AND THE SABBATH DAY

21.1. The light of nature shows that there is a God who has lordship and sovereignty over all, that he is good and does good to all, and that he ought therefore to be feared, loved, praised, prayed to, trusted in, and served with all the heart, and with all the soul, and with all the might. But the acceptable way of worshiping the true God has been instituted by himself, and so limited by his own revealed will, that he may not be worshiped according to the imaginations or devisings of men, or the suggestions of Satan, or under any visible representation, or any other way not commanded in Holy Scripture.

21.2. Religious worship is to be given to God alone—Father, Son, and Holy Spirit. It is not to be given to angels, saints, or any other creature. And since the Fall, worship is not to be given except through a mediator, nor is it to be given through any mediator other than Christ.

21.3. Prayer with thanksgiving is a special part of religious worship and is required by God of all men. In order that prayer may be accepted, it is to be made in the name of the Son, by the help of his Spirit, and according to his will. Prayer is to be offered with understanding, reverence, humility, fervency, faith, love, and perseverance. If vocal, it must be offered in a language that is understood.

21.4. Prayer is to be made for things that are lawful and for all kinds of men now alive or who will live at a later time. But it is wrong to pray for the dead or for those known to have committed the sin unto death.

21.5. The various elements of the ordinary religious worship of God are the reading of the Scriptures with reverence; the sound preaching and conscientious hearing of the Word in obedience to God, with understanding, faith, and reverence; the singing of psalms with grace in the heart; and the proper administration and worthy receiving of the sacraments instituted by Christ. Also, on special occasions and at appropriate times, there are other elements of worship, namely, religious oaths, vows, solemn fasts, and thanksgivings. These are to be used in a holy and devout manner.

21.6. Under the gospel, neither prayer nor any other part of religious worship is now limited to—or made more acceptable by—any particular place where it is performed or toward which it is directed. On the contrary, God is to be worshiped everywhere in spirit and truth. He should be worshiped daily in families, and privately by individuals, and with greater solemnity in public worship services. Such worship services are not to be carelessly or willfully neglected or forsaken when God by his Word or his providence calls people to them.

21.7. As it is the law of nature that, in general, a proper proportion of time ought to be set apart for the worship of God, so God in his Word—by a positive, moral, and perpetual commandment binding all men in all ages—has specifically appointed one day in seven for a Sabbath to be kept holy to him. From the beginning of the world to the resurrection of Christ, the appointed Sabbath was the last day of the week. Beginning with the resurrection of Christ, the Sabbath was changed to the first day of the week, which in Scripture is called the Lord's day, a day to be continued until the end of the age as the Christian Sabbath.

21.8. This Sabbath is then kept holy to the Lord when men, after due preparation of their hearts and arranging of their common affairs beforehand, not only observe a holy rest, all the day, from their own works, words, and thoughts concerning their everyday occupations and recreations, but also devote the whole time to the public and private exercises of God's worship and to the duties of necessity and mercy.

## Chapter 22

# LAWFUL OATHS AND VOWS

22.1. A lawful oath is a part of religious worship, in which—on an appropriate occasion—the person taking the oath solemnly calls upon God to witness what he asserts or promises and to judge him according to the truth or falsehood of what he swears.

22.2. The name of God is the only name by which men should swear, and they should do so with all holy fear and reverence. Therefore, to swear vainly or rashly by that glorious and fearful name, or to swear at all by any other thing, is sinful and to be abhorred. Yet since, in matters of weight and great importance, an oath is warranted by the Word of God under the new testament as well as under the old, therefore, a lawful oath ought to be taken when imposed in such matters by lawful authority.

22.3. Whoever takes an oath ought to consider seriously the great importance of such a solemn act, and in doing so should affirm nothing but what he himself is fully convinced is the truth. A person may bind himself by oath only to what is good and just, what he believes to be such, and what he is able and resolved to perform.

22.4. The oath is to be taken in the plain and usual sense of the words, without equivocation or mental reservation. It cannot oblige a person to sin, but when it is taken in matters which are not sinful, it obligates performance of the oath even though it may hurt. The oath is not to be violated even though it is made to heretics or unbelievers.

22.5. A vow is similar in nature to a promissory oath and ought to be made with the same religious care and be performed with the same faithfulness.

22.6. A vow is to be made only to God and not to any created being. In order for it to be acceptable, it is to be made voluntarily, out of faith and conviction of duty, either from thankfulness for mercy or from the desire to obtain what we lack. By taking a vow we bind ourselves more strictly to necessary duties, or to other things to the extent that they contribute to the performance of these duties.

22.7. No one may vow to do anything forbidden in the Word of God or anything which would hinder the performance of any duty it commands. No one may vow to do anything for which he has no ability and for which he has no promise of ability from God. With respect to these things, Roman Catholic monastic vows of perpetual single life, professed poverty, and regular obedience—far from being steps to higher perfection—are in fact superstitious and sinful snares, in which no Christian may entangle himself.

## Chapter 23

# THE CIVIL AUTHORITIES

23.1. God, the supreme Lord and King of all the world, has ordained civil authorities to be, under him, over the people for his own glory and the public good. For this purpose he has armed them with the power of the sword for the defense and encouragement of those who are good, and for the punishment of those who do evil.

23.2. It is lawful for Christians to hold public office when called to it. In such office they ought especially to maintain piety, justice, and peace, according to the wholesome laws of each commonwealth. For that purpose they may now, under the new testament, lawfully wage war upon just and necessary occasion.

23.3. Civil authorities may not assume to themselves the administration of the Word and sacraments, or the power of the keys of the kingdom of heaven, nor should they interfere in any way in matters of faith. Yet, as caring fathers, it is the duty of civil authorities to protect the church of our common Lord without giving preference to any denomination of Christians above the rest—doing so in such a way that all church authorities shall enjoy the full, free, and unquestioned liberty of carrying out every part of their sacred functions without violence or danger. As Jesus Christ has appointed a regular government and discipline in his church, no law of any commonwealth should interfere with, prevent, or hinder their proper exercise among the voluntary members of any denomination of Christians, according to their own profession and belief. It is the duty of civil authorities to protect the person and good name of all their people in such an effective manner that no person be allowed, either in the name of religion or of unbelief, to offer any indignity, violence, abuse, or injury to any other person whatever. They should also take care that all religious and ecclesiastical assemblies be held without interference or disturbance.

23.4. It is the duty of people to pray for those in authority, to honor them, to pay them taxes or other revenue, to obey their lawful commands, and to be subject to their authority for the sake of conscience. Neither unbelief nor difference in religion makes void the just and legal authority of officeholders nor frees the people—church authorities included—from their due obedience to them. Much less does the Pope have any power or jurisdiction over civil authorities in their domains or over any of their people, nor can he deprive them of their domains or lives if he shall judge them to be heretics or on any other pretense whatever.

## Chapter 24

# MARRIAGE AND DIVORCE

24.1. Marriage is to be between one man and one woman. It is not lawful for any man to have more than one wife, or for any woman to have more than one husband, at the same time.

24.2. Marriage was ordained for the mutual help of husband and wife, for the increase of mankind with legitimate offspring and of the church with godly children, and for the prevention of sexual immorality.

24.3. It is lawful for all sorts of people to marry who are able to give their intelligent consent. Yet it is the duty of Christians to marry only in the Lord. Therefore, those who profess the true reformed religion should not marry unbelievers, Roman Catholics, or other idolaters; nor should Christians be unequally yoked by marrying those who are notoriously wicked in their way of living or hold to damnable heresies.

24.4. Marriage ought not to take place between persons who are within the degrees of close relationship by blood or by marriage forbidden by the Word. Such incestuous marriages can never be made lawful—so that such persons may live together as man and wife—by any law of man or by the consent of the parties involved.

24.5. Adultery or fornication committed after engagement, if detected before marriage, gives valid reason to the innocent party to break the engagement. In the case of adultery after marriage it is lawful for the innocent party to seek a divorce and after the divorce to remarry just as if the offending party were dead.

24.6. Although the corruption of mankind is such that people are apt to seek arguments to justify unwarranted separation of those whom God has joined together in marriage, nothing but adultery or such willful desertion as cannot be remedied by the church or the civil authorities is sufficient cause to dissolve the bond of marriage. In such cases a public and orderly procedure is to be observed, and the persons concerned are not to be left to their own wills and discretion in their own case.

## Chapter 25

# THE CHURCH

25.1. The catholic (that is, universal) church, which is invisible, consists of all the elect who have been, are, or shall be gathered into one, under Christ its head. This church is his bride, his body, and the fullness of him who fills all in all.

25.2. The visible church, which is also catholic (that is, universal) under the gospel (that is, not confined to one nation, as it was before under the law), consists of all those throughout the world who profess the true religion, together with their children. It is the kingdom of the Lord Jesus Christ, the house and family of God, outside of which there is no ordinary possibility of salvation.

25.3. To this universal, visible church Christ has given the ministry, oracles, and ordinances of God for the gathering and perfecting of the saints, in this life, to the end of the age. For this purpose he makes these means effectual by his own presence and Spirit, according to his promise.

25.4. This universal church has been sometimes more and sometimes less visible. Particular churches, which are members of this universal church, are more or less pure to the extent to which the doctrine of the gospel is taught and embraced, the ordinances are administered, and public worship is performed more or less purely in them.

25.5. The purest churches on earth are subject to both mixture and error, and some have so degenerated that they have become no churches of

Christ at all, but rather synagogues of Satan. Nevertheless, there shall always be a church on earth to worship God according to his will.

25.6. There is no other head of the church but the Lord Jesus Christ. Nor can the Pope of Rome be its head in any sense.

## Chapter 26

# THE COMMUNION OF SAINTS

26.1. All saints—who are united to Jesus Christ their head by his Spirit and by faith—have fellowship with him in his graces, sufferings, death, resurrection, and glory. And, being united to one another in love, they participate in each other's gifts and graces and are obligated to perform those public and private duties which lead to their mutual good, both inwardly and outwardly.

26.2. It is the duty of professing saints to maintain a holy fellowship and communion in the worship of God and in performing such other spiritual services as help them to edify one another. It is their duty also to come to the aid of one another in material things according to their various abilities and necessities. As God affords opportunity, this communion is to be extended to all those in every place who call on the name of the Lord Jesus.

26.3. The communion which the saints have with Christ does not make them in any way partakers of the substance of his Godhead, or in any respect equal with Christ. To affirm either is irreverent and blasphemous. Nor does their fellowship with one another as saints take away or infringe upon any person's title to, or right to, his own goods and possessions.

## Chapter 27

# THE SACRAMENTS

27.1. Sacraments are holy signs and seals of the covenant of grace. They were directly instituted by God to represent Christ and his benefits and to confirm our relationship to him. They are also intended to make a visible distinction between those who belong to the church and the rest of the world, and solemnly to bind Christians to the service of God in Christ, according to his Word.

27.2. In every sacrament there is a spiritual relationship, or sacramental union, between the visible sign and the reality signified by it, and so it happens that the names and effects of the one are attributed to the other.

27.3. The grace which is exhibited in or by the sacraments, rightly used, is not conferred by any power in them. Neither does the efficacy of a sacrament depend on the piety or intention of him who administers it, but rather on the work of the Spirit and on the word of institution, which contains (together with a precept authorizing its use) a promise of benefit to worthy receivers.

27.4. There are only two sacraments ordained by Christ our Lord in the gospel: baptism and the Lord's supper. Neither sacrament may be administered by any person except a minister of the Word, lawfully ordained.

27.5. With regard to the spiritual realities signified and exhibited, the sacraments of the old testament were essentially the same as those of the new testament.

## Chapter 28

# BAPTISM

28.1. Baptism is a sacrament of the new testament, ordained by Jesus Christ, by which the person baptized is solemnly admitted into the visible church. Baptism is also for him a sign and seal of the covenant of grace, of his ingrafting into Christ, of regeneration, of forgiveness of sins, and of his surrender to God through Jesus Christ to walk in newness of life. By Christ's own appointment, this sacrament is to be continued in his church until the end of the age.

28.2. The outward element to be used in this sacrament is water, with which the person is to be baptized in the name of the Father, and of the Son, and of the Holy Spirit. Baptism is to be performed by a minister of the gospel, lawfully called to that office.

28.3. Dipping of the person into the water is not necessary. Baptism is rightly administered by pouring or sprinkling water on the person.

28.4. Not only those who personally profess faith in and obedience to Christ, but also the infants of one or both believing parents, are to be baptized.

28.5. Although it is a great sin to despise or neglect this ordinance, nevertheless, grace and salvation are not so inseparably connected with it that a person cannot be regenerated or saved without it. Neither is it true that all who are baptized are undoubtedly regenerated.

28.6. The efficacy of baptism is not tied to that moment of time when it is administered. Nevertheless, by the right use of this ordinance, the grace promised is not only offered but really exhibited and conferred by the Holy Spirit to all (whether adults or infants) to whom that grace belongs, according to the counsel of God's own will, in his appointed time.

28.7. The sacrament of baptism is to be administered only once to any person.

## Chapter 29

# THE LORD'S SUPPER

29.1. Our Lord Jesus, on the night when he was betrayed, instituted the sacrament of his body and blood, called the Lord's supper. It is to be observed in his church until the end of the age for the perpetual remembrance of the sacrifice of himself in his death, for the sealing of all the benefits of that death unto true believers, for their spiritual nourishment and growth in him, for their increased commitment to perform all the duties which they owe to him, and for a bond and pledge of their fellowship with him and with each other as members of his mystical body.

29.2. In this sacrament Christ is not offered up to his Father, nor is any real sacrifice made at all for the forgiveness of the sins of the living or the dead. Instead, this sacrament is only a commemoration of that one sacrifice by which Christ offered himself on the cross once for all. The sacrament is a spiritual offering of the highest praise to God for that sacrifice. So, the Roman Catholic sacrifice of the mass (as they call it) is a detestable insult to Christ's one and only sacrifice, which is the only propitiation for all the sins of his elect.

29.3. In this ordinance the Lord Jesus has appointed his ministers to declare his word of institution to the people; to pray and consecrate the elements of bread and wine, and so set them apart from a common to a holy use; and to take and break the bread, take the cup, and give both to the communicants, and to partake with the congregation. But they are not to give the elements to any who are not then present in the congregation.

29.4. Private masses—or receiving this sacrament from a priest or anyone else, alone—are contrary to the nature of the sacrament and to the institution of Christ. For the same reasons it is forbidden to deny the cup to the members of the congregation, to worship the elements, to lift them up or carry them around for adoration, or to reserve them for any supposedly religious use.

29.5. The visible elements in this sacrament, when they are properly set apart for the uses ordained by Christ, have such a relationship to Christ crucified that they are sometimes called—truly, but only sacramentally— by the name of the things they represent, namely, the body and blood of Christ. This is true even though in substance and nature they still remain truly and only bread and wine, as they were before.

29.6. The doctrine which teaches that the substance of the bread and wine is changed into the substance of Christ's body and blood (commonly called transubstantiation) by the consecration of a priest, or in any other way, is repugnant not only to Scripture but even to common sense and reason. It overthrows the nature of the sacrament and has been and is the cause of many superstitions and gross idolatries.

29.7. Worthy receivers of this sacrament, outwardly partaking of its visible elements, also inwardly by faith—really and indeed, yet not physically but spiritually—receive and feed upon Christ crucified and all the benefits of his death. The body and blood of Christ are not physically in, with, or under the bread and wine; yet in this ordinance the body and blood of Christ are present to the faith of believers in as real a spiritual sense as the bread and wine are to their physical senses.

29.8. Even if ignorant and wicked men receive the outward elements in this sacrament, yet they do not receive that which is signified by the elements. Rather, by their unworthy coming to the sacrament, they are guilty of the body and blood of the Lord, to their own damnation. Therefore, all ignorant and ungodly people, because they are unfit to enjoy fellowship with the Lord, are also unworthy to participate in the Lord's supper. As long as they remain unworthy, they cannot be admitted to the Lord's table or partake of the holy mysteries without great sin against Christ.

## Chapter 30

# CHURCH DISCIPLINE

30.1. The Lord Jesus, as King and Head of his church, has appointed a government in it, to be administered by church officers, distinct from the civil authorities.

30.2. To these church officers he has committed the keys of the kingdom of heaven. For this reason they have authority to retain and to remit sins, to shut the kingdom against the unrepentant both by the Word and by censures, and to open it to repentant sinners by the ministry of the gospel and by releasing from censures, as the occasion requires.

30.3. Church discipline is necessary for reclaiming and gaining fellow Christians who are guilty of offenses, for deterring others from committing similar offenses, for purging the leaven which might infect the whole lump, for vindicating the honor of Christ and the holy profession of the gospel, and for averting the wrath of God which might justly fall on the church if it should allow his covenant and its seals to be profaned by notorious and obstinate offenders.

30.4. For the better attaining of these purposes, the officers of the church are to proceed by admonition, by suspension from the sacrament of the Lord's Supper for a time, and by excommunication from the church, according to the nature of the offense and the degree of the person's guilt.

## Chapter 31

# SYNODS AND COUNCILS

31.1. For the better governing and further edifying of the church, there ought to be such assemblies as are commonly called synods or councils. Overseers and other rulers of particular churches, by virtue of their office and the power which Christ has given them for edification and not for destruction, have authority to appoint such assemblies and to convene together in them as often as they judge it expedient for the good of the church.

31.2. Synods and councils have authority ministerially to decide controversies of faith and cases of conscience, to set down rules and directions for the better ordering of the public worship of God and the government of his church, and to receive and authoritatively act on complaints of maladministration in the church. If the decrees and decisions of these synods and councils are in accordance with the Word of God, they are to be received with reverence and submission, not only because of their agreement with the Word, but also because of the authority by which they are decided, as being an ordinance that God has appointed in his Word.

31.3. Since apostolic times, all synods and councils, whether general or particular, may err, and many have erred. Therefore, they are not to be made the rule of faith or practice, but are to be used as a help in regard to both.

31.4. Synods and councils are to handle or conclude nothing but what pertains to the church. They are not to intermeddle in civil affairs which concern the state, except by way of humble petition in extraordinary cases, or by way of advice, for satisfaction of conscience, if they are required to do so by the civil authority.

## Chapter 32

# THE STATE OF MEN AFTER DEATH, AND THE RESURRECTION OF THE DEAD

32.1. After death, the bodies of men decay and return to dust, but their souls, which neither die nor sleep, having an immortal existence, return immediately to God, who gave them. The souls of the righteous are then made perfect in holiness and received into the highest heavens, where they behold the face of God in light and glory as they wait for the full redemption of their bodies. The souls of the wicked are cast into hell, where they remain in torments and utter darkness as they are kept for the judgment of the great day. Scripture recognizes no other place except these two for the souls which have been separated from their bodies.

32.2. At the last day those who are alive shall not die but shall be changed. All the dead shall be raised up with their selfsame bodies, and no other (although with different qualities), which shall be united again with their souls forever.

32.3. By the power of Christ the bodies of the unjust shall be raised to dishonor. The bodies of the just shall be raised to honor by his Spirit and brought into conformity with Christ's own glorious body.

*Chapter 33*

# THE LAST JUDGMENT

33.1. God has appointed a day in which he will judge the world in righteousness by Jesus Christ, to whom all power and judgment has been given by the Father. In that day not only shall the apostate angels be judged, but also shall all people who have ever lived on earth appear before the judgment seat of Christ in order to give an account of their thoughts, words, and deeds, and to receive judgment according to what they have done in the body, whether good or evil.

33.2. God's purpose in appointing this day is to manifest the glory of his mercy in the eternal salvation of the elect, and the glory of his justice in the damnation of the reprobate, who are wicked and disobedient. On that day the righteous shall go into everlasting life and receive that fullness of joy and refreshing which shall come from the presence of the Lord; but the wicked, who do not know God and who do not obey the gospel of Jesus Christ, shall be cast into eternal torments and be punished with everlasting destruction from the presence of the Lord and from the glory of his power.

33.3. As Christ would have us to be absolutely convinced that there will be a day of judgment, both to deter all men from sin and to give greater consolation to the godly in their adversity, so will he have that day unknown to men, that they may shake off all carnal security, may always be watchful—because they do not know at what hour the Lord will come—and may always be prepared to say, "Come, Lord Jesus. Come quickly. Amen."